Guilt-Free Living

Guilt··Free Living

How to know when you've done enough

. . . . .

Robert Jeffress

Tyndale House Publishers, Inc.
WHEATON, ILLINOIS

Unless otherwise indicated, Scripture quotations are taken from the *New American Standard Bible,* © 1960, 1962, 1963, 1968, 1971, 1972, 1973, 1975, 1977 by The Lockman Foundation. Used by permission.

Scripture quotations marked KJV are taken from the *Holy Bible,* King James Version.

Scripture verses marked TLB are taken from *The Living Bible,* copyright © 1971 owned by assignment by KNT Charitable Trust. All rights reserved.

Scripture quotations marked NIV are taken from the *Holy Bible,* New International Version®. Copyright © 1973, 1978, 1984 by International Bible Society. Used by permission of Zondervan Publishing House. All rights reserved. The "NIV" and "New International Version" trademarks are registered in the United States Patent and Trademark Office by International Bible Society. Use of either trademark requires permission of International Bible Society.

Library of Congress Cataloging-in-Publication Data

Jeffress, Robert, 1955-
 Guilt-free living : how to know when you've done enough / Robert Jeffress.
  p. cm.
 Includes bibliographical references.
 ISBN 0-8423-1724-4 (softcover)
 1. Guilt—Religious aspects—Christianity. 2. Satisfaction—Religious Aspects—Christianity.
3. Contentment—Religious aspects—Christianity. I. Title.
BJ1471.5.J44 1995
241'.4—dc20
                                                                        94-42408
                                                                        CIP

Printed in the United States of America

00 99 98 97 96
5   4   3   2   1

For Amy

*"An excellent wife,
who can find?
For her worth is
far above jewels."*

Proverbs 31:10

CONTENTS

ONE
Enough Is Enough 1

TWO
The Enemies of Guilt-Free Living 19

THREE
Guilt-Free Time Management 33

FOUR
Guilt-Free Work 51

FIVE
Guilt-Free Relaxation 71

SIX
Guilt-Free Money Management 91

SEVEN
Guilt-Free Marriage 115

EIGHT
Guilt-Free Parenting 141

NINE
Guilt-Free Friendships 165

TEN
Guilt-Free Bible Study 185

ELEVEN
Guilt-Free Praying 205

TWELVE
Guilt-Free Ministry 227

Notes 243

. . . . .

CHAPTER 1

Enough Is Enough

G O then, eat your bread in happiness, and drink your wine with a cheerful heart; for God has already approved your works (Eccles. 9:7).

"Pastor, I enrolled in this discipleship training group in order to be encouraged. But the more the teacher talked, the guiltier I felt. As he talked about quiet times, witnessing, Scripture memory, and Bible study, I realized how far off the mark I was."

A woman in our church was telling me about her situation. She was a divorced senior adult, having severe medical problems herself, and was responsible for her mother, who was suffering from Parkinson's disease. Yet she was concerned that she was not "doing enough" in her Christian life. Her constant care of her mother did not allow her to attend church regularly, nor was she able to have an uninterrupted quiet time every morning. She had managed to arrange some part-time help to take care of her mother so that she could attend this discipleship class on Sunday nights. She had come to the church looking for encouragement. Instead, she left with a wheelbarrow full of guilt.

As her pastor, I faced a dilemma. I surely didn't want to minimize the importance of these disciplines in her Christian life. What if we all used our difficult circumstances (and who doesn't have some?) to rationalize our failures in these and other areas of life? On the other hand, this woman had just about all of the stress she could handle. Somehow it did not seem right that Christians, of all people, should be responsible for loading more guilt on her already buckling shoulders.

This woman's situation is not unique. Many of us are laboring under a load of illegitimate guilt—guilt about our spiritual life, our marriage, our children, our finances, our time management (or lack of it!), and a dozen other areas in life. And, unfortunately, the church is often the source of, rather than the cure for, much of this guilt. Those of us who are preachers and writers are constantly telling people they need to do *more:*

> *more* effort to improve relationships
> *more* pounds to lose
> *more* time to spend in the spiritual disciplines
> *more* money to be saved (or given away)
> *more* people to win to Christ

If this gnawing sensation that you haven't done enough is your all-too-common companion, you are being robbed of one of the greatest pleasures in life—a pleasure that most Christian books would not dare address. A thrill that most radio talk shows could only discuss in the late night hours. A sensation so exhilarating that you would think it immoral, if not illegal!

This book will introduce you to the pleasure, the sensation, the thrill of . . . *closure.* Before you put this book down in disappointment, let me explain what I mean.

Closure is the feeling that you have done everything that needs to be done at that time. Therefore, you are free to relax and enjoy yourself without any guilt. (Sounding better, isn't it?) Can you recall a time you have ever felt that way?

If you are a homemaker, have you ever been able to look around your house and say, "The dishes are clean, the clothes are washed, the children are in bed, and I am free to sit and read an article I want to read, or just sit and stare"? *That is closure.*

If you are a student, can you recall the relief you felt after finishing a major project or a term paper? You could have done more, but the project is in reasonably good shape, and now it's time to celebrate. You're ready to enjoy closure.

Or, for those of you in the business world, when was the last time you have been able to say that you have made every call that needs to be made, you have finished the major projects that need to be completed, and your company is enjoying reasonable success? You have done everything you could do. That is an example of closure.

I remember one rare time like that last spring. Our church had just completed a successful revival, we had finished an involved long-range plan for our church, and I had just completed two major writing assignments. I felt I had actually done enough. Oh, sure, there were more things I *could* have done, but I really did not feel that I had to. What a feeling!

God wants us to experience the joy of closure in our relationships, in our work, and in our spiritual life. And the key to enjoying such closure is to understand clearly what God requires in these areas and to reject the unrealistic expectations of others, which lead to oppression. And this book is designed to help you do just that.

A dentist in our church has a most unusual hobby—polevaulting. Every evening after a busy day of drilling and billing, he goes home and spends several hours trying to vault over a metal bar. But he is never satisfied. As soon as he has successfully cleared the bar at one height several times, he does something utterly ridiculous (at least to me): He raises the bar! And this only increases his frustration level, as he spends several more weeks trying to successfully clear the bar at that height. Then what does he do? You guessed it; he raises the bar again!

If my dentist friend were able to really relax and enjoy himself, I could understand. But this guy is the type who gets so wrapped up in his hobby that he continually berates himself for not being able to vault higher.

As he described his hobby and accompanying frustrations to me one day at lunch, I thought about the number of people who are frustrated with their lives because of some invisible bar they keep raising in their minds—unrealistic, self-imposed expectations about their work, or relationships, or even their spiritual lives.

For example, consider the busy mother with small children who feels like her house needs to look like the cover of *Good Housekeeping*. Or the teenage athlete who chastises himself for not being another Michael Jordan. Or parents who wish their family was more like the Waltons than the Simpsons.

No, there is nothing wrong with setting goals for ourselves— unless those goals are unrealistic and rob us of the satisfaction in life that God wants us to enjoy. The purpose of this book is to help you eliminate those unrealistic, self-imposed expectations about different life areas so that you can enjoy the satisfaction that God intends for you to have.

A "DANGEROUS" DOCTRINE

When is the last time you read a Christian parenting book that said, "Relax. You're doing everything as a parent that you can do. You are not responsible for the decisions your children ultimately make"? Can you recall a sermon in which the preacher said, "Some of you need to read your Bibles less and enjoy life more"? Can you imagine attending a Christian financial seminar in which the speaker said, "You have saved enough money and given enough away. Go out and blow the rest on something you want to do"? Can you picture a Christian marriage counselor saying, "Quit worrying about your marriage. What you're experiencing in your relationship is normal. You are doing everything as a wife (or husband) that you need to do"?

We find it hard to believe that we ever could or should reach such conclusions. Everything inside us wars against such contentment. After all, doesn't this kind of thinking lead to slothfulness, stagnation, and ruin? Yes, there are excesses to be avoided when we talk about guilt-free living. But I believe that the benefits far outweigh the potential dangers.

Let me illustrate how the removal of a negative emotion can be beneficial. When the Golden Gate Bridge was completed in 1937, it was the world's largest suspension bridge to date. The project cost the government more than $77 million. During the construction of the first section of the bridge, very few safety devices were used. The result was that twenty-three men fell to their deaths in the icy water below. Something had to be done. So the world's largest safety net, costing more than $100 thousand, was stretched beneath the workmen. What was the result of this safety net? Did the men become more careless? No, the work on the second phase of the bridge went 25 percent faster than on the first phase. Why? Because the fear of falling had been removed. The men were able to work more confidently.

Fear and guilt are closely related. Neither emotion is constructive. Instead, they both sap our emotional and spiritual strength. If we can legitimately (and biblically!) remove fear and guilt from our life, the result does not have to be disobedience or slothfulness; it can be a more spiritually productive life.

In some ways the "doctrine" of guilt-free living is comparable to the doctrine of the eternal security of the believer. Those of us who believe in eternal security are willing to argue at the drop of a hat with those who don't. Yet we are somewhat reluctant to teach on the subject too often. We perceive the doctrine of eternal security as a somewhat "dangerous" doctrine. If a Christian is constantly told that he is secure in Christ Jesus, regardless of what he does, won't that promote a disobedient lifestyle? Yet it would be wrong to neglect such an important biblical doctrine due to the fear that some might misunderstand or misapply that truth.

I think of the experience of my own father, who is now at home with the Lord. He became a Christian while in the army, through the influence of a chaplain from a denomination that did not believe in the security of the believer. Although my father later became a Baptist, he never was able to resolve the doubts he had about his own position in Christ. The result of those doubts was not a more obedient lifestyle but a life filled with anxiety and fear—fear that kept him from reaching his full spiritual potential. Fear and guilt don't motivate—they paralyze.

As we will see in the next chapter, not all guilt is bad. There are some Christians who *should* feel guilty. Not every Christian is meeting his obligations as a parent, or reading his Bible enough, or managing his money correctly, or fulfilling his marriage responsibilities. The fact is that we all fall short in many of these areas. Yet the questions remain: Does God have a reasonable standard in each of these areas that we can realistically meet? And once we meet those standards, can we enjoy a sense of closure—the assurance that we have done enough?

I believe the answer to both of those questions is yes. And this book will show you how to experience closure in the major areas of your life.

Is Closure Biblical?

In his book *When All You've Ever Wanted Is Not Enough,* Harold Kushner tells the story about a rabbi who commented to one of the members of his congregation, "Whenever I see you, you're always in a hurry. Tell me, where are you running all the time?" The man answered, "I'm running after success, I'm running after fulfillment, I'm running after the reward for all my hard work." The rabbi responded, "That's a good answer if you assume that all those blessings are somewhere ahead of you, trying to elude you, and if you run fast enough, you may catch up with them. But isn't it possible that those blessings are behind you, that they are looking for you, and the more you run, the harder you make it for them to find you?"[1]

Many years ago there lived a king who spent the better part of his life running after money, power, fame, pleasure, and even spirituality. But at the end of his life he appeared to be a broken and unfulfilled man. His name was Solomon, and the book of Ecclesiastes is a journal of his observations about life, death, and eternity. There are some fine conservative theologians who try to dismiss the first eleven chapters of this book as the humanistic observations of a man clearly out of fellowship with God. Only when we get to chapter 12 ("Remember also your Creator in the days of your youth") do we see a "spiritual" perspective on life, they claim.

But a closer evaluation of these first eleven chapters reveals that Solomon was right on target with his observations, though some are difficult for us to accept.

For example, consider his comments about death:

> For I have taken all this to my heart and explain it that righteous men, wise men, and their deeds are in the hand of God. Man does not know whether it will be love or hatred; anything awaits him. It is the same for all. There

is one fate for the righteous and for the wicked; for the good, for the clean, and for the unclean; for the man who offers a sacrifice and for the one who does not sacrifice. As the good man is, so is the sinner; as the swearer is, so is the one who is afraid to swear. This is an evil in all that is done under the sun, that there is one fate for all men. (Eccles. 9:1-3)

"How can that be?" we ask. "Doesn't the Bible teach that there are two possible fates for men: heaven and hell?" Yes, but Solomon was not focusing on the eternal but the present. The fact is that we all die: the righteous and the unrighteous alike. Regardless of what awaits us on the other side of death, our time here is limited.

In light of our impending departure from this planet, what should be our response? Now, hold on to your hat! This is going to surprise you. Solomon does not say, "Therefore, since you are rapidly marching toward the grave,

"Read your Bible more.
Win more people to Christ.
Work harder.
Give more."

Instead, Solomon advises, "Go then, eat your bread in happiness, and drink your wine with a cheerful heart; for God has already approved your works" (9:7). Amazing, isn't it? This guy must have been out of fellowship when he penned these words, we imagine. After all, that philosophy sounds disturbingly similar to the pagan refrain "Eat, drink, and be merry, for tomorrow we die." Yet a closer observation of this verse and its context reveals that these words are not a wholesale call to hedonism. Solomon does place some boundaries around this philosophy.

First, Solomon erects *spiritual* boundaries around our enjoyment of life. He writes, "Let your clothes be white all the time, and let not oil be lacking on your head" (Eccles. 9:8). Obviously, Solomon was not advocating that women wear flowing white dresses all the time or men walk around with a head filled with Brylcreem (I'm showing my age) or mousse. In Solomon's day white garments represented festivity. Bathing or anointing oneself with oil was considered luxurious (much like a bubble bath today). But I believe Solomon had more in mind here than simply our dress and personal hygiene. White garments often symbolized purity. Solomon is saying that our behavior should be wrapped in righteousness. Oil is often used in the Bible as a symbol of the Holy Spirit's power. Thus, Solomon is saying that all pleasure should take place within the parameters of godliness.

Second, Solomon places *moral* boundaries around our enjoyment of life. The fact that we will soon die should cause us to enjoy our sexuality to the fullest while we are still able. There will be no sex beyond the grave. But Solomon says that we are limited to enjoying sensual pleasure with our mate: "Enjoy life with the woman whom you love all the days of your fleeting life which He has given to you under the sun; for this is your reward in life, and in your toil in which you have labored under the sun" (Eccles. 9:9). However, these pleasures within marriage are to be limitless. More will be said about this when we come to the chapter "Guilt-Free Marriage."

Third, Solomon places *vocational* boundaries around our enjoyment of life. Throughout the book of Ecclesiastes there is a tension between work and pleasure. On the one hand, Solomon points to the futility of worshiping work:

> So I hated life, for the work which had been done under the sun was grievous to me; because everything is futility and striving after wind. Thus I hated all the fruit of my labor for which I had labored under the sun, for I must

leave it to the man who will come after me. And who knows whether he will be a wise man or a fool? Yet he will have control over all the fruit of my labor for which I have labored by acting wisely under the sun. This too is vanity. (Eccles. 2:17-19)

And yet, here, Solomon extols the value of work. "Whatever your hand finds to do, verily, do it with all your might; for there is no activity or planning or wisdom in Sheol where you are going" (9:10). Translation: Whatever you are going to accomplish, you'd better do it now, because when your time is over, *it's over!* The fact that we will one day die, or the Lord might return at any moment, is no excuse for slothfulness.

But Solomon says that once we have met our spiritual, moral, and vocational obligations, we are free to enjoy life to the fullest. It is possible to have your work "approved by God." Yet most of us have a difficult time accepting that possibility.

Recently, I read a book about a long legal battle between humorist Art Buchwald and Paramount Studios over money the studio supposedly owed Buchwald for a movie idea. According to Buchwald's contract, as soon as the movie made back its cost, he was to start receiving a percentage of the profits. But the studio utilized an accounting device called "a rolling break-even point." That is, through some accounting tricks, they kept raising the break-even point of the movie so that Buchwald never could receive any of the profits. Although the movie made tens of millions of dollars, technically it never "broke even," and therefore, the writer was denied the fruit of his labor.

As I read that story, I thought what a perfect analogy it was of life in general. No matter how hard we work in our jobs, our spiritual lives, our relationships, we can never seem to do enough. Someone keeps moving the "break-even point."

But I believe God's Word teaches that there is a break-even

point—a standard—for every area of life. Once we meet that standard, we can enjoy satisfaction, relaxation, and the assurance of God's approval.

We find the principle of closure throughout the Bible. Moses experienced it:

> And he erected the court all around the tabernacle and the altar, and hung up the veil for the gateway of the court. Thus Moses *finished* the work." (Exod. 40:33, emphasis mine) And it came about, when Moses *finished* writing the words of this law in a book until they were complete. . . . (Deut. 31:24, emphasis mine)

Solomon experienced it:

> Thus Solomon *finished* the house of the Lord and the king's palace, and *successfully completed* all that he had planned on doing in the house of the Lord and in his palace. (2 Chron. 7:11, emphasis mine)

Nehemiah experienced it:

> So the wall was *completed* on the twenty-fifth of the month Elul, in fifty-two days. (Neh. 6:15, emphasis mine)

Jesus experienced it:

> It is *finished.* (John 19:30, emphasis mine)

Paul experienced it:

> I have fought the good fight, I have *finished* the course, I have kept the faith. (2 Tim. 4:7, emphasis mine)

God's people are to experience it:

> My people shall be *satisfied* with My goodness. (Jer. 31:14, emphasis mine)

Still not convinced that closure is a sensation that God wants us to enjoy? Then consider God's two greatest acts in human history: Creation and the Atonement.

TGIS: THANK GOD IT'S SATURDAY

After God spent six days creating the sun, the moon, the oceans, the stars, plant life, animal life, and man, we find these concluding words in Genesis 1:

> And God saw all that He had made, and behold, it was very good. And there was evening and there was morning, the sixth day. Thus the heavens and the earth were *completed*, and all their hosts. And by the seventh day God *completed* His work which He had done; and He *rested* on the seventh day from all His work which He had done. Then God blessed the seventh day and sanctified it, because in it He *rested* from all His work which God had created and made. (Gen. 1:31–2:3, emphasis mine)

Notice the repetition of the words *completed* and *rest*. God was able to *complete* the grandest project imaginable. And once he finished that project, he rested from the act of creation. And he experienced *satisfaction* from his work.

In those six days, did God create everything that he could have created? I think not. There is no end to the galaxies, the planets, the animals, the plants, and even the types of humans

God could have created (why limit it to two?). Yet, after six days, God said, "Enough is enough! What I have done is great!"

Some of you are probably thinking, *Of course, God was able to complete his work and enjoy satisfaction. He's* **God!** But what about us poor mortals? Haven't we been condemned to a life of endless labor? Aren't our efforts always going to be less than satisfactory?

God's reason for resting on the seventh day was not for his benefit, but for ours. He was trying to teach us the divine principle of closure. As we will see in chapters 4 and 5, God's design for our lives is that at least once a week we experience closure in our work. That is, we say, "Enough. I have completed the work God has given me to do. It is finished!"

The principle of closure is also seen in the life and work of Jesus Christ. Throughout his thirty-three years of life on this planet, Jesus had one goal: to accomplish the work God had for him to complete. That singular, driving purpose is seen in Jesus' words in John 4:34: "My food is to do the will of Him who sent Me, and to accomplish His work." When one thinks of all of the needs Jesus must have seen around him—the disease, the heartaches, the broken relationships, the myriad of unsaved lives—coupled with the limited time he knew he had on earth, we can only imagine the urgency Jesus could have felt.

And yet, as you examine Jesus' life and ministry, you notice that he was never in a hurry. He walked everywhere he went. His schedule was never too busy to enjoy some lighthearted moments with his disciples, some playful times with children, or even a good party like the wedding at Cana. Jesus did not heal every sick person, raise every dead person, or even convert every sinner. Yet, when he hung on the cross he was able to say, "It is finished."

Theologians tell us that the Greek word *tetelestai* (translated "it is finished") was an accounting term that could be translated "paid in full." The word described a debt that had been satisfied. When Jesus died on the cross, he paid the obligation of our sin.

No one would want to diminish the significance of Christ's atoning work on the cross. Yet I think we would make a mistake to limit Jesus' meaning of "It is finished" to the Atonement. The word *tetelestai* was also a general word that referred to the completion of an assignment. When a servant completed his job, he would report to his master, *"Tetelestai"* ("I have finished the work you've given me to do").

I believe this is what Jesus was saying on the cross. Although he had not fulfilled every ministry opportunity available, he had completed the work God had given him to do. That sense of completion is what allowed Jesus to say, "I glorified Thee on the earth, having accomplished the work which Thou hast given Me to do" (John 17:4). Please notice those final words, "which Thou hast given Me to do." Jesus was not claiming that all work was finished, but that *his* work was finished. He had successfully completed his assignment.

That sense of completion and satisfaction need not be limited to the first and second persons of the Godhead. I believe that God wants all of us to experience closure in every area of our lives. And the way to experience that closure is to understand God's requirements for each of these areas and reject man-made expectations that lead to oppression. In this book we are going to look at closure in three major life areas and their related topics:

GUILT-FREE LIFE MANAGEMENT
Guilt-Free Work
Guilt-Free Relaxation
Guilt-Free Time Management
Guilt-Free Money Management

GUILT-FREE RELATIONSHIPS
  Guilt-Free Marriage
  Guilt-Free Parenting
  Guilt-Free Friendships

GUILT-FREE SPIRITUALITY
  Guilt-Free Bible Study
  Guilt-Free Praying
  Guilt-Free Ministry

"If I had my life to live over . . ."

The following words were supposedly written by an anonymous friar in a Nebraska monastery, late in life:

> If I had my life to live over again, I'd try to make more mistakes next time.
>
> I would relax, I would limber up, I would be sillier than I have been this trip.
>
> I know of very few things I would take seriously.
>
> I would take more trips. I would be crazier.
>
> I would climb more mountains, swim more rivers and watch more sunsets.
>
> I would do more walking and looking.
>
> I would eat more ice cream and less beans.
>
> I would have more actual troubles, and fewer imaginary ones.
>
> You see, I'm one of those people who lives life prophylactically and sensibly hour after hour, day after day. Oh, I've had my moments, and if I had to do it over again, I'd have more of them.
>
> In fact, I'd try to have nothing else, just moments, one after another, instead of living so many years ahead each day. I've been one of those people who never goes any-

where without a thermometer, a hot-water bottle, a gargle, a raincoat, aspirin, and a parachute.

If I had to do it over again I would go places, do things, and travel lighter than I have.

If I had my life to live over I would start barefooted earlier in the spring and stay that way later in the fall.

I would play hooky more.

I wouldn't make such good grades, except by accident.

I would ride more merry-go-rounds.

I'd pick more daisies.[2]

At this stage in our lives, some of us cringe at those observations. "Life is serious business!" we protest. Should we really waste it on ice cream, merry-go-rounds, and daisies? But when you reach the end of your life and look back over your years, do you imagine that you will say, "Oh, I wish I had worked longer hours at the office" or "If only I had saved more money" or "I would give anything to have made better grades"? Probably not.

I remember hearing television newswoman Barbara Walters's observation about her greatest lesson in life. She said, "There are no dress rehearsals in life. Only one performance, and this is it."

As Solomon reflected on his life, he reached a similar conclusion. Regardless of what happens in eternity, we all have one chance in this life, so we had better savor every moment. "For the living know they will die; but the dead do not know anything, nor have they any longer a reward, for their memory is forgotten. Indeed their love, their hate, and their zeal have already perished, and they will no longer have a share in all that is done under the sun. Go then, eat your bread in happiness, and drink your wine with a cheerful heart; for God has already approved your works" (Eccles. 9:5-7).

Are you ready to unshackle yourself from the unrealistic expectations of others? Do you desire to experience the freedom that comes from God's approval of your life? If so, this book is for you! Our first step on the road to a guilt-free life is to identify and eliminate the three enemies of guilt-free living.

. . . . .

CHAPTER 2

The Enemies of Guilt-Free Living

IS guilt bad? Should we avoid guilt at any cost? Can we truly live a guilt-free existence? Newspaper columnist Ann Landers offers an interesting "insight" about guilt:

> One of the most painful, self-mutilating, time- and energy-consuming exercises in human experience is guilt. . . . It can ruin your day—or your week or your life—if you let it. It turns up when you do something dishonest, hurtful, tacky, selfish, or rotten. . . . Never mind that it was the result of ignorance, stupidity, laziness, thoughtlessness, weak flesh, or clay feet. You did wrong and the guilt is killing you. Too bad. But be assured the agony you feel is normal. . . . Remember guilt is a pollutant and we don't need any more of it in the world.[1]

Apparently, Ann Landers subscribes to what I call "Big-Bird Theology." If you have preschoolers in your home, like I do, the television program *Sesame Street* is probably a part of your family's daily ritual. Whenever that giant yellow character Big Bird makes a mistake, he comforts himself by saying, "Everybody makes mistakes."

My daughter, Julia, eagerly adopted that rationale for her own misbehavior. For a period of time, whenever she was disobedient, she would offer the excuse "Well, Dad, *everybody* makes mistakes." Dad was less than impressed. And I believe that God is less than impressed with our efforts to rationalize our failures and our disobedience by simply saying, "Well, we are only human. What can you expect?"

When I write about guilt-free living, I am not advocating the Ann Landers or Big Bird approach to sin and guilt. Man has been trying to deny, excuse, and cover over his sin from the beginning of time. But the Bible clearly teaches that apart from Jesus Christ we are guilty before God and deserving of punishment. The apostle Paul makes that point in his sweeping indictment of humanity, found in Romans 3:10-12: "There is none righteous, not even one; there is none who understands, there is none who seeks for God; all have turned aside, together they have become useless; there is none who does good, there is not even one."

Paul, quoting from the Old Testament, claims that no one is righteous. The term *righteous* simply means to be in a right standing before God. In other words, all have fallen short of God's standards.

Suppose three men were standing on the coast of California and, in a moment of insanity, decided they would try to swim to Hawaii. The first swimmer is able to go thirty miles before succumbing to exhaustion. The second man swims ten miles before he is forced to stop. The third man, however, only swims one mile before sinking to the bottom of the ocean. The difference between distances covered is considerable. But compared to the distance to Hawaii, the differences are inconsequential.

It is the same in our relationship with God. We see a great spectrum of differences in human behavior. For example, our local newspaper carried the story about a father who tortured and murdered his four infant and preschool children. One can hardly imagine a more despicable act. On the other end of the spectrum we see a man like Walt Disney—a father who brought laughter and happiness to millions of children. Two very different men. But compared to the righteousness of God, such differences in human behavior are negligible. All of us have fallen woefully short of God's standards.

Thus, as we begin this study of guilt-free living, we must understand the reality of guilt. The reason many people feel guilty is because they *are* guilty. And as we will see in the next section, there is only one way to remedy our guilt before God.

Yet, the premise of this book is that once we have taken that initial step of receiving God's forgiveness for our many failures, it is possible to enjoy a guilt-free existence.

Let's review for a moment what we saw in the last chapter:

1. One of the greatest pleasures in life is closure—the feeling that we have done enough.

2. Many godly people are not enjoying closure. Instead, they are driven to do more—more in their relationships, more in their work, and more in their spiritual lives. They think that "more" is the key to the satisfaction, fulfillment, and approval from God they so desperately want. And yet the drive for more many times causes the blessings of satisfaction and fulfillment to elude us. (Remember the story about the rabbi's conversation with one of his members?)

3. Although many of us have a difficult time believing

we can ever do enough in any area of life, the Bible clearly teaches the principle of closure. We saw it in Ecclesiastes 9:7. We also saw closure demonstrated in the two greatest acts of history: the Creation and the Atonement. When God finished creating the world, he said, "Enough. I will rest and enjoy what I have done." When Christ reached the end of his earthly life, he was able to say with great satisfaction, "I have accomplished the work You have given Me to do."

4. The key to experiencing closure is to meet God's requirements in each life area and reject unrealistic expectations that lead to oppression. Jesus' singular purpose in life was to do God's will. He repeatedly rejected the man-made and oppressive requirements of the Pharisees. More will be said about this in the next section.

"LITE MESSAGES"

When I first preached about guilt-free living in our church, I had a variety of responses from our members. After the sermon, in which I presented the contents of the previous chapter, a deacon who had a short announcement to make began with this observation about my message. He said, "I am sure you have heard of 'lite colas' and 'lite beers.' Recently I saw a cartoon advertising the 'lite church.' On the sign in front of the church were these inducements to attend: Hour Services in Only Forty-five Minutes; Only Six Commandments Observed; Tithes Reduced to 7.5 Percent."

After a polite chuckle from the congregation, the deacon added the zinger. "And pastor, if I have ever heard a 'lite' sermon, that was it!" The crowd roared with laughter, and I joined in with them.

True, this message was far different from most sermons I had preached. And as I discovered through the week, the concept of guilt-free living is not only foreign but is actually threatening to a few. Some Christians are masochistic about their worship experience. They come to the service wanting the pastor to really "step on their toes." The more he abuses them, the better they feel. A good tongue-lashing from the preacher serves as modern-day penance for these people. After hearing a fiery message preached, some will approach the minister and say, "Thanks, I needed that" (like the old Aqua Velva commercial). Now understand they have *no* intention of changing their behavior because of the message. They reason that sitting through such a message has some atoning power of its own. They've done their part by just listening to it!

But let a pastor stand up and suggest that once Christians have met God's requirements they can relax and enjoy life, and the saints get restless. "That's not what we pay this guy for. He's supposed to tell us how lousy we are." Frankly, that was the reaction I faced from some when I introduced this concept of guilt-free living.

However, most of our congregation responded positively to this idea. They said things like "I have never heard that idea before" or "That is exactly what I needed to hear." One young woman who was just recovering from an emotional breakdown said to me, "It is as if God himself were speaking to me through that message." I immediately realized I was addressing a felt need when I talked about guilt-free living. And the reason is obvious. The church is filled with conscientious Christians who are trying to please God. Many of them are doing a marvelous job of balancing the demands of work, family, and spiritual life. And yet when they come to church looking for encouragement, they are rebuked for not doing enough. To offer the possibility of guilt-free living to a group of faithful Christians in an active church is a little like selling lemonade in the middle of the Sahara. It is a rare commodity.

A few of the congregation were skeptical. They really wanted to believe that what I was saying was true. Yet, the idea that one can ever do enough in any area of life is refuted by a "still small voice" inside that says, "You can never do enough. You will never be able to please God." I will admit that most of us have such a voice within us. For some the voice is louder than for others. But is that voice from God? If not, where does it originate?

I believe there are three reasons most Christians have difficulty enjoying closure in their lives. These are the three enemies of guilt-free living that I want us to explore in this chapter.

ENEMY #1: UNRECEIVED GRACE

Many Christians do not truly understand what Christ accomplished for them on the cross. Therefore, they think that they can in some way add to what Christ has already done for them. These people believe that if they will just read their Bible more, or give more, or become a better parent or mate, they can either merit God's love or at least make him love them a little more.

It's easy to understand why some people believe they must earn God's grace. First of all, our own fallen nature is too prideful to admit that we are incapable of earning God's approval. We want to play some part in the redemptive process. For the last two thousand years mankind has been trying to hang a sign on the cross that says, Necessary—But Not Enough. Yet the Bible clearly states that God "saved us, not on the basis of deeds which we have done in righteousness, but according to His mercy, by the washing of regeneration and renewing by the Holy Spirit" (Titus 3:5). Did you catch that? God's grace is *completely* unconnected to our actions.

But I think it would be wrong to blame our inability to accept God's grace entirely on our fallen nature. Life itself conditions us to link performance with acceptance. As children we learn early that if we are compliant and obedient, we gain our parents' approval. As students we quickly learn the relationship between good grades and our teachers' acceptance. We also learn that excellence in extracurricular activities translates into popularity among our peers.

When we advance into the workplace, we immediately are taught that good performance results in pay raises and promotions. And even when we become parents and grandparents, we learn that our children's and grandchildren's love and acceptance is often based on what we do for them.

My point is not that any of this is necessarily wrong. But I am simply demonstrating why so many people have difficulty accepting the fact that God's love has nothing to do with performance. That concept violates human experience.

In summary, God's grace means that there is nothing you can do to make God love you any more or any less than he already does. If you are a Christian, you already have God's unconditional love and acceptance. Do you believe that? If you have difficulty with that idea, you do not fully comprehend the benefits of God's grace. And you will find it impossible to enjoy a guilt-free life.

ENEMY #2: UNRESOLVED CONFLICTS

A closely related reason some people cannot enjoy a guilt-free life is because of unresolved conflicts in their lives: with God, with themselves, or with others. Instead of confronting those conflicts, they many times work harder or expend more effort in another life area that is easier for them to handle. On a simplistic level, if they have a weight problem and cannot fit into their clothes, they can (a) work on reducing their weight or (b) buy bigger clothes. The second choice, (b), is preferred by most! Notice how that works with guilt.

One reason some people cannot enjoy a guilt-free life is because of an unresolved conflict *with God.* A proud person who will not admit his sin to God tries to atone for his transgression in a way other than confession and repentance. He may throw himself into community service projects. If he accomplishes enough good for other people, he thinks that might compensate for his spiritual deficiency.

A Christian I know could not get enough of God's Word. He was always studying, listening to tapes, attending seminars. And he was very critical of fellow Christians who were not "in the Word." Later, it was revealed that this man was involved in a number of immoral relationships. Intense, never-ending Bible study was the way he compensated for his unresolved conflict with God.

Sometimes the unresolved conflicts that hinder a guilt-free life are with *other people.* For example, consider a woman who is deeply bitter toward her husband over something that happened many years ago. The bitterness has turned the marriage into nothing but an emotional shell. Instead of resolving that bitterness, the woman tries to compensate by being a model mother for her children. Yet she never feels that she can do enough for her children.

I know some Christians who either harbor tremendous bitterness toward other people, or they themselves are guilty of divisiveness and slander—yet they are some of the most faithful workers in the church. They have deluded themselves into thinking that they can overlook these conflicts by hyper-participation in church activities. Yet they can never seem to do enough.

By the way, Jesus clearly taught that spiritual activity can never compensate for unresolved conflicts with others. Jesus taught the importance of resolving personal conflicts rather than ignoring them or trying to compensate with spiritual activity:

> If therefore you are presenting your offering at the altar, and there remember that your brother has something against you, leave your offering there before the altar, and go your way; first be reconciled to your brother, and then come and present your offering. (Matt. 5:23-24)

Sometimes the unresolved conflicts that rob us of closure are *within.* Our inability to reconcile ourselves to personal failure causes us to work harder in other areas of life. For example, a divorced father unable to accept the failure of his marriage pours himself into his children. He is obsessed with being a perfect father—attending every activity, making sure his children have every opportunity, providing for their every need and want. Yet he still feels that he is not doing enough as a father.

I think about the life of former president Lyndon Johnson. Growing up in abject poverty in south central Texas and suffering the ridicule of his peers, Johnson determined that he would never be poor. Unable to make peace with his past, he was relentless in his desire to succeed, to the point of sacrificing his own health.

Are there conflicts in your life that you have tried to ignore rather than confront? Conflicts with God, with others, or even with yourself? If so, you may try to overcompensate for those conflicts in other areas of life and never experience a guilt-free existence.

ENEMY #3: UNREALISTIC EXPECTATIONS

Perhaps the most lethal of all of the enemies of guilt-free living is unrealistic expectations. Remember the formula for a guilt-free life? We can only enjoy closure in life by meeting God's requirements for each area of life and by rejecting unrealistic expectations of others that lead to oppression. In this book, I want to explain what I believe are God's simple requirements for each of these areas. But that is not enough. We need to be equally committed to rejecting those unrealistic expectations that we or others have manufactured. Such expectations will keep us bound in a web of guilt.

Sometimes those unrealistic expectations are obvious: the young businessman who is disappointed that he is not a millionaire by age twenty-five; a single mom trying to juggle the demands of work and home who feels guilty for not being "disciplined" enough to spend an hour exercising every day like some of her friends; or the pastor in a deteriorating town of two thousand people who wonders why his eight-hundred-seat sanctuary is not filled every Sunday.

Other times these expectations don't seem so ridiculous, but they are just as dangerous. For example, consider the salesman who sets an unusually high quota for himself—he is going to triple what he did last year. Great goal! (In fact, he formulated this goal while attending a Sunday evening class at his church on goal setting). But is that goal realistic? And even if it can be done, what personal cost is involved? In his case, such a goal wars against a guilt-free life. He is already a workaholic (notice that the first goal he thought of was work related). His inability to say "enough" in his work has many ramifications. First, he cannot enjoy relaxation, because he is constantly thinking he should be making another call. Even on a rare occasion that he might spend on vacation, or with his family, he is not really there, but thinking about his job. He cannot enjoy closure. But the damage does not stop there.

This lack of closure in one area of life produces a chain

reaction in other areas. His obsession with "more" in his work forces him to neglect other areas, like his family, his friendships, and his spiritual life. So he finds himself in a double bind. On one hand, he can never feel he is doing enough in his work. And that lack of closure in his work precludes his meeting very real obligations in other areas, resulting in legitimate guilt.

Where do such unrealistic expectations originate? They can spring from within—either our inability to truly receive God's grace, or unresolved conflicts with God, others, or ourselves. But many times these unrealistic expectations come from external sources—friends, families, or even the church. What are some of these unrealistic expectations that rob Christians of a guilt-free life? Look at several examples of unrealistic expectations that will be addressed in subsequent chapters.

1. Time management

I have attended numerous Christian seminars and read dozens of books on time management. To listen to some of these experts speak, you get the idea that every moment of your life should have profound significance. God is pictured as a divine efficiency expert, sitting on his throne with a giant Day-Timer, recording how well you use your time. In chapter 3 we will explore this idea further.

2. Money management

Christians are also bombarded with advice about how to manage their money. We are told that we should be saving thousands of dollars each year for our children's education and our own retirement. However, we are warned that we should not go into debt—owing money is a sin. And at the same time, we are encouraged to give an increasing percentage of money to support God's work! No wonder so many Christians are suffering from floating anxiety about their finances! In chapter 6 we will examine what God's Word *really* says (and doesn't say) about saving, debt, and giving.

3. Marriage

Listen carefully to some of the advice being given about marriage. One well-known Christian speaker talks about the "fireworks" he and his wife experience behind the bedroom door every night. Yet most Christians do not sustain such pyrotechnics in their relationship day after day, year after year. Should they feel guilty? If you and your mate are not enjoying wedded bliss every moment, are you falling short of God's expectations for your marriage? Some of the Christian myths about marriage are guilty of inflating our expectations about marriage and causing needless discontent. In chapter 7, we are going to attempt to explode those myths.

4. Prayer

Think about your prayer life for a moment. How many times have you heard stories about the great saints from yesteryear who prayed for hours at a time? Do those stories make you feel as guilty as they do me? We are inclined to think, *Maybe God is not answering my prayers because I haven't spent long enough praying.* Yet the responsibilities of work, family, ministry, and even recreation make it difficult to carve out large blocks of time for prayer. Being unable to meet such a standard, many Christians quit praying altogether.

I believe God wants to free us from unrealistic expectations that enslave us to guilt. How do I know that? Look at the way Jesus dealt with the Pharisees. The Pharisees were noted for having developed a whole body of tradition outside of the Old Testament that they believed to be equal to the authority of God's Word. For example, they took the fourth commandment about the Sabbath and added thirty-nine more laws to interpret it! In talking about our complicated judicial system today, someone has observed that we have more than fifty thousand laws to interpret the Ten Commandments.

Jesus vigorously condemned the Pharisees for their restrictive theology. He said that the Pharisees "tie up heavy loads, and lay them on men's shoulders; but they themselves are unwilling to move them with so much as a finger. . . . But woe to you, scribes and Pharisees, hypocrites, because you shut off the kingdom of heaven from men; for you do not enter in yourselves, nor do you allow those who are entering to go in" (Matt. 23:4, 13).

Not only did Jesus condemn the Pharisees, but he refused to allow their expectations to govern his life. Notice how Jesus handled their criticism concerning the Sabbath.

> At that time Jesus went on the Sabbath through the grainfields, and His disciples became hungry and began to pick the heads of grain and eat. But when the Pharisees saw it, they said to Him, "Behold, Your disciples do what is not lawful to do on a Sabbath." But He said to them, "Have you not read what David did, when he became hungry, he and his companions; how he entered the house of God, and they ate the consecrated bread, which was not lawful for him to eat, nor for those with him, but for the priests alone? Or have you not read in the Law, that on the Sabbath the priests in the temple break the Sabbath, and are innocent?" (Matt. 12:1-5)

Jesus kept pointing the Pharisees back to the Word of God. "Have you not read . . . ?" Jesus refused to become a slave to human expectations. Instead he patterned his life on the simple requirements of God's Word. And he was able to enjoy a guilt-free existence on earth.

I believe God wants each of us to enjoy that same kind of

freedom. And in the following chapters we are going to examine what God's Word requires in these different life areas. Understanding those simple requirements will give us the ability to reject the unrealistic expectations of others that rob us of fulfillment.

Few life areas produce more guilt than the one we will consider first.

. . . . .

CHAPTER 3

Guilt-Free Time Management

O NE day a woodsman bought a brand-new ax. The first day he was able to chop down twenty trees. With each passing day he worked longer and harder while chopping down fewer trees. A friend wandered by and suggested, "Why don't you sharpen your ax?" The woodsman replied, "I don't have time. I've got to chop down more trees!"

I thought about that story last Saturday afternoon as I sat in the church office trying to finish some work. I had spent the day polishing my two messages for Sunday, praying for the services, visiting the hospitals, calling all of the visitors from the previous Sunday, and dictating some correspondence. When four o'clock in the afternoon rolled around, I still had a pile of work to complete. But something suddenly compelled me to pack up my briefcase and vacate the premises. I drove to the corner deli, purchased a cup of white Belgian cappuccino (with cream and cinnamon) along with an oversized chocolate chip cookie, and sat outside to enjoy the bright, crisp Saturday afternoon. For

GUILT-FREE LIVING

the next thirty minutes I did nothing except eat, drink, and watch the cars go by.

Was that an efficient use of time? Part of me said no. There were still more "trees" to chop down. But another part of me said that this was the most important thing I could be doing right then—not because this brief respite would make me more productive later, but simply because there is more to life than duty. Sometimes the best use of time is to spend it on something other than work, family, or (here's a heretical thought) even spiritual pursuits. Life is not just to be endured but enjoyed.

In this book we are addressing the subject of guilt-free living. And no area of life is more prone to produce more guilt feelings than the way we manage our time. Some of the guilt feelings are legitimate. Our failure to be good stewards of the limited time God has given us translates into disordered lives, unfinished tasks, and unrealized dreams. However, some of the guilt we feel about our time management comes from unrealistic expectations about our time (as well as our lives).

In this chapter we are going to explore the two seemingly contradictory perspectives about time found in the Bible. Then we are going to explode the major myth about time that causes so much illegitimate guilt among Christians. Finally, we will explain some practical time management suggestions that will allow you to "go then, eat your bread in happiness, and drink your wine with a cheerful heart."

COMPLIMENTARY OR CONTRADICTORY?

Before we can experience guilt-free time management, we need to gain God's perspective about time. Remember, the key to guilt-free living is to understand God's requirements for the particular life area and then reject unrealistic expectations that lead to oppression. What does God say about our time?

Search the pages of Scripture, and you will find one consistent truth about time that is applied in two very distinct and seemingly contradictory ways. The truth is this: Time is a limited resource that should be treasured.

The brevity of life is a theme that appears like a flashing beacon throughout the Bible. James says that our life is like a mist that appears for a little while and then vanishes (James 4:14). In the oldest of all the psalms, Moses, in the twilight years of his life, reflects on life's brevity:

> Thou dost turn man back into dust, and dost say, "Return, O children of men." For a thousand years in Thy sight are like yesterday when it passes by, or as a watch in the night. Thou hast swept them away like a flood, they fall asleep; in the morning they are like grass which sprouts anew. In the morning it flourishes, and sprouts anew; toward evening it fades, and withers away. (Ps. 90:3-6)

Moses uses two images to illustrate the shortness of our lives: dust and grass. Our physical bodies are a collection of chemicals and particles that will one day return to the ground. People have all kinds of grand ideas about what they want done with their body after they die. Some want to be buried, others cremated, others have decided to donate their organs to science. One of my relatives has made me promise to scatter his ashes over Grand Teton Mountain. But regardless of what we do, our physical bodies will soon return to the ground.

Moses also uses the image of grass to demonstrate the brevity of time. In the morning the grass springs up new. But toward the evening, it fades and dies. This verse has always bothered me because it does not seem accurate. Grass does not grow and die in a single day. Yet that is exactly Moses' point. Compared to eternity, our life is over in less than a day.

Pretty depressing, isn't it? We all have an assigned number of years, days, hours, minutes, and seconds. And they are relentlessly ticking away. TICK . . . Tick . . . tick . . .

What should be our response to the brevity of life? Despair? Hedonism? No, Moses' prayer is that God will "teach us to number our days, that we may present to Thee a heart of wisdom" (90:12). I like the way *The Living Bible* translates verse 12: "Teach us to number our days and recognize how few they are; help us to spend them as we should." Because time is brief, we should manage it as a valuable commodity.

In his book *When All You've Ever Wanted Isn't Enough*, Rabbi Harold Kushner has proposed what he calls the "instant coffee theory of life." He says that when you open a new jar of coffee, you tend to dole it out in generous portions because you have a jar filled with coffee. But halfway down the jar you tend to become a little more conservative. You realize the jar isn't going to last forever. By the time you reach the bottom of the jar, you find yourself measuring your portions very carefully, reaching into the corners of the jar for every last grain.

We tend to treat time that way. When we are young, we tend to be careless about how we spend our lives. We think we can afford to waste time—after all, we have an entire life in front of us. We feel as if we will live forever. But about halfway through life, it begins to dawn on us that we are not going to live forever, and we begin to reevaluate every area of life—our relationships, our work, our values. This often leads to what we call a "midlife crisis."

By the time we reach our fifties and sixties, we realize that we have fewer years ahead of us than behind us. And toward the end of our lives we ask, "How did life go by so quickly?"[1]

The biblical perspective about time is very simple: Our time on earth is brief and therefore very valuable. Thus, we should carefully decide how we are going to allocate our time.

PANIC OR PLEASURE?

To some people such a concept does not alleviate guilt, it only induces more guilt, even panic! "Since the clock is ticking, since my life is like a mist that is about to evaporate or a blade of grass that is about to wither away, I'd better make sure that I spend every moment doing something 'significant.'" Several years ago, I read a time-management book that said you should order your life around this question: What is the most productive thing I could be doing this minute? Try living that way for a day!

I recently read this paraphrase of Psalm 23 that expresses that panic that the ticking clock can cause:

> *The clock is my dictator, I shall not rest.*
> *It makes me lie down only when exhausted.*
> *It leads me to deep depression.*
> *It hounds my soul.*
> *It leads me in circles of frenzy for activity's sake.*
> *Even though I run frantically from task to task,*
> *I will never get it all done,*
> *For my "ideal" is with me.*
> *Deadlines and my need for approval, they drive me.*
> *They demand performance from me, beyond the limits of my*
>   *schedule.*
> *They anoint my head with migraines.*
> *My in-basket overflows.*
> *Surely fatigue and time pressure shall follow me all the days*
>   *of my life,*
> *And I will dwell in the bonds of frustration forever.*
>   *—Marcia K. Hornok*

Does God really intend for us to live that way? Is the proper response to life's brevity full-blown panic? I will have to admit that in times past I have responded that way. Both of my parents died of cancer within a few years of each other. Both were relatively young. I went into a period of deep depression after their deaths. Most people thought my despair was due to the loss of the two most significant people in my life. And certainly part of it was. But I was also distraught over the realization that my days were also numbered.

This realization led to two seemingly contradictory conclusions. One was that I ought to eliminate all "time wasters": television, sleeping late on Saturday mornings, entire days where I seemed to accomplish nothing except visiting with other people, and so on. Instead, I would be "productive." I would invest my remaining time on earth in "eternal things."

The other equally strong sensation was more the Solomonic conviction that life was futile anyway, and therefore, I should spend my life pursuing those things that would bring pleasure. I remember having the strong urge to empty my savings account and take an around-the-world luxury vacation with my wife.

During that period of time I read in the *Wall Street Journal* about the early retirement of Peter Lynch, one of Wall Street's whiz kids. Lynch was only in his forties but had also lost both of his parents. Lynch observed that once you have lost both of your parents "your life forever loses the flavor of immortality." Thus, the realization of life's brevity caused Lynch to leave his chosen profession in order to spend time with his family and enjoy life. Although it would have been impossible for me to do the same (Wall Street tycoons tend to have more options than the rest of us), the desire to do so was very strong.

Thus, the realization of life's brevity led to two very distinct desires: (1) to invest time wisely and (2) to spend time freely.

Which application is "correct"? Actually, both are. Although none of us likes contradictions, all truth is held in tension. And that is true about time management.

Time *is* a limited resource. Some of it should be invested in spiritual pursuits: strengthening our spiritual life, leading other people to faith in Jesus Christ, ministering to the needs of others. Many of Jesus' parables teach that one day we will give an account to God for the money, time, and opportunities he has entrusted to us (see Matthew 19). In 2 Corinthians 5:10 Paul reminded us that "we must all appear before the judgment seat of Christ, that each one may be recompensed for his deeds in the body, according to what he has done, whether good or bad." The judgment described here is a judgment all Christians will face. It is not a judgment that will determine our eternal destiny—that has already been decided. This is a judgment of rewards.

And what will be the standard that determines our rewards? "According to what he has done, whether good or bad." Our rewards will be based on our activity in this life. The word translated "bad" does not refer to moral transgressions. Instead, the word means "worthless." This is a judgment based on our stewardship of our lives. Have we spent time pursuing the eternal? Or has our time been consumed by trivial pursuits? Ralph Waldo Emerson once said, "The best use of time is to spend it on something that will outlast it."

THE MYTH OF ETERNAL SIGNIFICANCE

Certainly one reason some people feel guilty about their time management is due to the lack of any eternal pursuits in life. But an equally lethal cause of guilt is what I call "the myth of eternal significance." You have probably heard this sermon many times—I know I have (I've even preached it). "There are only two things that will last for eternity: God's Word and people.

Thus, the way to make your life count for eternity is to spend it instilling God's Word in people." Pretty convicting, wouldn't you say?

The only problem is that most people must discount the value of about 98 percent of their lives, according to that viewpoint. We spend most of our time doing essential things that have little to do with "instilling God's Word in the lives of people"—work, family responsibilities, civic duties, recreation, and other essentials of daily life.

Fortunately, as we will discuss further in the next chapter, the Bible does not draw such a fine distinction between the eternal and the temporal, or the sacred and the secular. God is interested in *all* aspects of our lives: our family, our work, our relaxation, as well as our spiritual pursuits. To equate wise time management with only "spiritual" pursuits is wrong and leads to unbearable guilt.

If my work is a sacred calling from God, could I not also make a case that my family is a sacred calling from God? If my secular work is an extension of God's kingdom program, isn't my family a part of that program as well? Why should I feel guilty about blowing an entire Saturday playing with my seven-year-old daughter in the park?

Or look at the area of recreation. God created this world for our enjoyment. Repeatedly in the creation account God reminds Adam that the world is "for you" (Gen. 1:29, 2:9). God took pleasure in creating a world for man's enjoyment. "And God saw all that He had made, and behold, it was very good" (Gen. 1:31). What is wrong with investing some of our time enjoying the world God has created for us? Isn't such enjoyment part of God's "eternal program"?

Not all of our time should be invested in the "eternal." Some of it should be spent on other life areas. And a portion of it should even be "wasted" on Friday night family outings, Saturdays in the park, Sunday afternoon naps, or simply watching the cars go by!

If you have a hard time with that idea, consider how you spend your money. Yes, the "wise" thing to do with your money might be to deposit all of it in the bank—preparing for the future. But most money-management experts will tell you that an even wiser approach is to allocate reasonable amounts to different life areas: food, clothing, contributions, recreation, as well as saving. Why? People who try to save too much money and shortchange other areas of life are likely to become so frustrated with the deficiencies in other areas of life that they "explode," go on a buying binge, and give up saving forever. The slow, consistent approach to investing yields much bigger returns in the long run.

That is also true about our time management. Trying to channel all of your time into one area—whether it is your spiritual life, work, recreation, or your family, is unwise. Rather, the goal of time management is to allocate properly your time into all the different life areas—work, family, friendships, recreation, as well as spiritual pursuits.

Yes, to meditate on the brevity of life is an important concept. You do "only go around once in life." However, such a truth should not induce guilt or promote hedonism. Instead, it should motivate us to properly balance our lives among all life areas.

GUILT-FREE TIME MANAGEMENT

So far we have seen that time is brief and, therefore, valuable. Some of it is to be invested in eternal pursuits; some of it is to be spent on those things that bring fullness to our lives: family, work, friendships, and recreation. How can we allocate our time wisely?

A myriad of books is available on the subject of time management. They address subjects like using the telephone efficiently, filing and retrieving information, how to make the most of meetings, how to use a calendar effectively, and on and on. Some of these books contain very simple and helpful tips for effective time use, such as:

- Use the time waiting in lines to read an article torn from a magazine rather than fume with impatience.
- Group appointments together. If the plumber is coming, schedule other repair people on the same day.
- Don't read your junk mail.
- Never climb stairs empty-handed.
- Use your TV time to mend clothes, rearrange a scrapbook, or do sit-ups.
- Pin socks together before putting them in the wash so that you don't have to search for matching pairs afterward.
- Buy birthday and anniversary cards for one year in one shopping trip.
- Schedule doctor's appointments at the beginning of the day so that you can be in and out before the doctor gets behind.

I could go on and on with tips like these. Certainly some of these tips are helpful. They can help us manage the mundane, but necessary, tasks of life more efficiently so that we are free to do those things we really want to do. But some of these suggestions cause *more* guilt. How? By inferring that every moment of life needs to be redeemed.

Does every moment of our lives need to be productive? Couldn't we see waiting in line as a momentary gift from God to catch our breath? Is it wrong to actually sit and watch a TV program without accomplishing anything? Do I really need to combine talking on the phone with some other activity like paying bills?

Instead of dealing with the minutiae of time-management techniques, I would like to concentrate on five general principles of time management guaranteed to reduce rather than induce guilt.

1. ESTABLISH YOUR OWN GOALS AND OBJECTIVES IN LIFE

The French critic and philosopher Nicolas Bolieau said, "He is most fatigued who knows not what to do." We tend to stereotype goal-oriented people as consistently uptight and guilt ridden, while the unambitious, live-for-today person is carefree. However, the opposite is often true. Those who have never developed clear objectives for their lives are more prone to stress and guilt than those who do.

For example, have you ever been on an automobile trip in which you got lost? Talk about stress! And then there is a surge of relief when you regain your bearings. In the same way, goals are compasses that give us direction in times of uncertainty. Frankly, the times I have felt most guilty about my time management have been those times when I had no clear-cut goals or I was ordering my life around someone else's objectives for my life.

Some people absolutely hate goal setting. When asked to set goals, they break out in a sweat. They feel guilty if they cannot formulate goals. Maybe that is why fewer than 3 percent of all Americans have clearly defined goals in life. If you are a person who has difficulty in setting goals, substitute "problem solving" for "goal setting."

What goals should I set (or problems should I solve)? Take an honest inventory of seven major life areas. On a scale of one to ten (ten = excellent; one = poor), how would you evaluate the following areas of your life?

1. Spiritual   1 2 3 4 5 6 7 8 9 10
2. Physical   1 2 3 4 5 6 7 8 9 10
3. Family   1 2 3 4 5 6 7 8 9 10
4. Vocational   1 2 3 4 5 6 7 8 9 10
5. Personal Growth   1 2 3 4 5 6 7 8 9 10
6. Social   1 2 3 4 5 6 7 8 9 10
7. Financial   1 2 3 4 5 6 7 8 9 10[2]

Are some areas of your life out of balance? For example, I might decide that I'm not spending enough quality time with my children. So, one of my objectives might be to spend more time with my family. To accomplish that objective I might set a specific goal to take each of my children out, one at a time, for an ice-cream cone once a week. Or maybe in evaluating my life, I see that my work is out of balance. So my objective might be to spend less time at work. One specific goal to accomplish that objective would be to finish all of my work by Saturday noon so that I can spend time with my family and devote Sundays to worship.

Remember, the purpose of goal setting is not to induce more guilt but to relieve the natural guilt we all feel when any of these seven life areas is out of balance. Goal setting is a tool that gives us direction in allocating our time.

For example, personal financial consultants often speak of "asset allocation." Depending on your age, you should invest a certain percentage of your money in stocks, another percentage in bonds, another portion in cash, some in real estate, and so on. If your portfolio is not aligned properly, you should not panic or feel guilty. Instead, you simply need to realign your investments. After all, the ultimate goal is a profitable portfolio. In the same way, we should honestly evaluate our life areas and the time we are investing in each one. If we are out of balance in any of these areas, we should not panic or feel guilty. Instead, we simply need to reallocate our time. The ultimate goal of such an exercise is a happy and fulfilling life.

2. SET "BOUNDARIES" FOR EACH LIFE AREA

Yes, some of the guilt we feel about our time is legitimate—such guilt may be a warning signal that we have not allocated our time properly. But some of the guilt we feel about time is the result of unrealistic expectations that we manufacture for ourselves or that others impose on us.

Too often we set unrealistic expectations for ourselves. I believe that to some extent we are all victims of the "American dream." All of our lives we have heard that there is no limit to what we can achieve if we work hard enough. We can have the highest income, the finest education, the biggest house, the most attractive spouse if we just exert enough effort. And I believe that such a myth fuels our time pressure. Our desire to be the best and have the best keeps us from experiencing closure.

The truth is that there will *always* be someone who has more than we have. For example, we have probably seen those lists of the one hundred wealthiest people in the world. Ninety-nine of those people are probably dissatisfied because there is someone who has more than they do. And the one person who is at the top of the list probably longs for something that one of the other ninety-nine has! One key to experiencing a guilt-free life is learning the secret of contentment. The apostle Paul said, "For we have brought nothing into the world, so we cannot take anything out of it either. And if we have food and covering, with these we shall be content" (1 Tim. 6:7-8). In other words, the key to contentment is limited expectations.

However, some of the time pressure we feel is due to the unrealistic expectations of others. In a former church I was visiting with several of our deacons. They were telling me about a particular family that had left our church before I became pastor. When I inquired why the family left the church, these men replied, "Because none of the staff attended the funeral for the mother's father." Since I was new to the church, I innocently asked, "Is it a requirement that staff members attend funerals for members' relatives?"

"Well, it is not a requirement," they said, "but it would have been nice for someone to have gone."

My initial response was, "Here's one more thing I need to add to my calendar (and my staff's calendar)." But the more I thought about it, I realized what an unrealistic expectation that was. Why hadn't these two deacons attended the funeral? Were they any busier than the staff?

If we are going to experience a guilt-free life, there comes a time when we must say, "Enough." Just as we saw in chapter one, there was a time when God the Father said, "Enough!" And there was a time when the Lord Jesus Christ said, "Enough." No, they had not accomplished everything they could have accomplished. God the Father could have created more planets; Jesus could have healed more sick people or saved more souls. But God placed boundaries around his responsibilities. And so should we. We can't have it all, and we can't *do* it all!

3. DON'T PROCRASTINATE—*DO IT NOW!*

But how can I keep those things I *must* do from overwhelming me? Mark Twain once offered this piece of advice: "Never put off till tomorrow what you can do . . . the day after tomorrow!" Unfortunately, too many people take this advice. And the result is a floating anxiety over tasks undone.

Why do people procrastinate? Psychologists tell us that the

number one reason for procrastination is the fear of failure. We won't start something because we are fearful that we will fail. The result is that we wait until the last moment, do a less-than-adequate job, and end up failing. Our fear has produced a self-fulfilling prophecy.

How can you avoid procrastination? Let me suggest several ideas. First, list all of your unfinished tasks, as well as other tasks you need to perform, in a spiral notebook. Such lists might include everything from scheduling a dentist appointment to completing a major report for your job. At this stage, don't worry about prioritizing that list. That will come later. When you finish a task, cross it off your list. As new tasks emerge, add them to your list. Just knowing that all of the things you need to do are written down *somewhere* will relieve a lot of guilt.

Second, break big jobs into small jobs. For example, one of your goals might be to clean out your garage. Such a job may seem frightening and overwhelming. Instead, divide your garage into four quadrants. Spend two hours on each quadrant for the next four Saturdays.

Third, whenever you are reluctant to begin a task, try boring yourself to death. That is, empty your mind of all thoughts. Sit and stare for a few minutes without doing anything. After a few minutes you will become so bored, you will be ready to start!

Finally, develop a reward system for those tasks you don't want to complete. For minor tasks at work, your reward might be a ten-minute coffee break. For major projects, it might be dinner out or the purchase of a new tie or dress.

4. Use a Daily To-Do List

When Charles Schwab was president of Bethlehem Steel Corporation, he asked a well-known consultant, Ivy Lee, to help him become more productive. "Show me a way to get more things done with my time, and I will pay you any fee within reason." Lee gave Schwab a piece of paper and said, "Write down the most important tasks you have to do tomorrow and number them in order of importance. When you arrive in the morning, begin at once on number one, and stay on it until it's completed. Recheck your priorities; then begin with number two. If any task takes all day, never mind. Stick with it as long as it's the most important one. If you don't finish them all, you probably couldn't do so with any other method, and without some system you'd probably not even decide which one was most important. Make this a habit every working day. When it works for you, give it to your men. Try it as long as you like. Then send me your check for what you think it's worth."

A few weeks later, Lee received a check for $25,000 and a note from Schwab saying that this was the most valuable advice he had ever received. Five years later, the Bethlehem Steel Corporation was the largest independent steel producer in the world. Schwab said that the $25,000 fee he paid Lee was the most valuable investment Bethlehem Steel had ever made.[3]

Just think, you got that advice for only the price of this book! Before you go to bed at night, or first thing in the morning, take a moment and jot down the six most important things you could accomplish that day (using your master list in the spiral notebook as a source of ideas). The next day, you will have a plan of action that will focus your energies on the most important tasks. Don't be discouraged if you don't complete the list. At least you will have concentrated your efforts on your highest priorities.

5. MAKE THE SABBATH A PART OF YOUR WEEKLY SCHEDULE

How can you keep the proper balance between work and rest in your weekly schedule? God has already devised a plan. It calls for six days of work and one of rest. This plan is so important that it made God's "top ten list" (a.k.a. the Ten Commandments). We will discuss the concept of the Sabbath further in the next two chapters.

All of these suggestions are simple, yet they will help you discover that perfect and individualized balance between duty and enjoyment in life. The Bible reminds us that time is a scarce and valuable gift. And someday we will give an account of our time to God. But we need to balance our expenditures of time among all life areas. Someone has written:

Make time to think—it is the source of power.
Make time to play—it is the key to freedom and
relaxation.
Make time to read—it is the gateway to knowledge.
Make time to worship—it washes the dust of earth from
your eyes.
Make time to help and enjoy friends—no other
happiness matches this.
Make time to love—if you don't it will fade away.
Make time to laugh and pray—these are the two things
that lighten life's load.
Make time to be alone with God—he is the Source of
everything.[4]

If you are like most people, the one area of your life that consumes most of your time is your work. In the next two chapters we will see how a proper balance between work and relaxation is essential to experiencing a guilt-free life.

. . . . .

CHAPTER 4

Guilt-Free
Work

WHEN the alarm clock goes off on Monday morning, the word that most closely describes my feeling is:

a. excitement

b. challenge

c. suicide

Would it surprise you to know that *c* is the answer preferred by most Americans? A number of studies about Americans' attitudes toward work all reveal the same facts. Eighty percent of those polled hate to get out of bed and go to work on Monday morning. Twenty-five percent display acute symptoms of job stress, such as absenteeism, substance abuse, divorce, physical illness, and poor quality work.[1]

The Psychology Department at Princeton conducted a study of Americans' attitude toward work. They interviewed 250,000 workers from four thousand companies, including every job category imaginable. The results? Eighty percent of those interviewed said they were dissatisfied with their job.

Despite the discontent so many people feel about their work, we appear to be working ourselves to death. You have heard the adage "Hard work never killed anyone." You'd better think again. We are witnessing a sharp rise in the number of job-related illnesses. In Japan *karoshi* (death from overwork) has become the second largest killer of the Japanese population, accounting for 10 percent of the deaths of working men in Japan. The victims are usually between the ages of forty and fifty and put in twelve- to sixteen-hour days over a number of years. Two-thirds of the deaths come from brain hemorrhages and one-third from myocardial infarction. These victims literally have worked themselves to death.[2]

In our country, a number of new job-related illnesses have appeared. A more familiar one is named Epstein-Barr virus, more commonly referred to as chronic fatigue syndrome. Nicknamed the "yuppie disease," it attacks mostly young, professional women. The symptoms include fever, swollen glands, and overpowering fatigue. Although the cause of this disease remains a mystery, researchers have found similarities between cocaine abuse and chronic fatigue syndrome. Researchers theorize that the same addictive behavior that causes cocaine abuse also characterizes workaholics, leading to a breakdown of the immune system. Additionally, workaholics experience a number of other stress-related illnesses, including ulcers, headaches, backaches, sleeping disorders, and high blood pressure.[3]

Why are we working so hard and enjoying it so little? Unfortunately, many people have allowed their attitudes about work to be shaped by culture and tradition rather than by God's Word. Our expectations about work, as a result, have reached one of two extremes. They have either been inflated to the point that our work can never satisfy us, or our attitudes toward our work have been so distorted by the cynicism of our culture that we view work as a curse rather than as a gift from God. To truly enjoy guilt-free work, we must gain a biblical perspective about it.

To reach a biblical perspective of work, we may need to review briefly the history of the American work ethic that has shaped our culture. As we will see, Americans have moved farther and farther away from the biblical view of work. The result is that our work has become a leading source of unresolved guilt.

THE DEVELOPMENT OF THE AMERICAN WORK ETHIC

In his book *The Leader*, Michael Maccoby discusses the five stages of the work ethic in American history. First, he explains the much maligned and often misunderstood *Puritan work ethic*. The Puritans' view of work was largely shaped by Calvinistic theology. Work—all work—was viewed as a sacred calling, which demanded their best efforts. The goal of work was not only prosperity but fulfillment of a divine mandate. Workers were partners with God in improving the physical, moral, and spiritual quality of life. Puritans saw no division between sacred and secular work. All work was an assignment from God. As Martin Luther said, "God even milks the cows through you." Excellence in work provided a very tangible way to glorify God.

The Puritan work ethic was replaced by the *craftsmen's ethic* in the era of Benjamin Franklin. No longer was work viewed as a sacred calling, nor was God seen as an integral part of work. Instead, work became highly individualized. The goal was no longer the betterment of society or the glory of God, but personal success. A distant deity, they believed, had set everything in motion, leaving workers responsible for their own success. Franklin's *Poor Richard's Almanac*, containing adages about diligence and persistence that would ensure success, was the craftsman's "bible." Such adages as "Early to bed and early to rise, makes a man healthy, wealthy, and wise" and "A stitch in time saves nine" usually related to the goal of labor—health, wisdom, and prosperity.

As the Industrial Revolution exploded on the American scene, the individual craftsmen's ethic of work gave way to the *entrepreneurial ethic*. Men like J. P. Morgan, John D. Rockefeller, and Andrew Carnegie were the heroes of this era. These men saw the goal of work as the maximization of profit. As they built their great monopolistic empires of wealth, they were not concerned with the people they ran over or the lives they crushed. The "bottom line" became the sole focus of their work. (For a modern-day expression of that philosophy, just look at the business section of your daily newspaper.) This ethic reminds me of comedienne Lilly Tomlin's comment "The trouble with the rat race is that even if you win, you're still a rat."

In our century, the *career ethic* replaced the entrepreneurial ethic. Since only a few could play at the entrepreneurial game, people decided that success in the system was even more important than accumulating great wealth. Climbing up the organization ladder—whether it was a corporation, the YMCA, or the government—was the goal. In order to ascend in the organization one needed to learn how to compromise and conform.

Today, our work ethic is best described as the *self-fulfillment ethic*. Work, material prosperity, even career advancement are secondary to the goal of personal fulfillment. The worker is looking for a nurturing work environment, job satisfaction, and self-actualization. In one interview, managers of corporations summed up the self-fulfillment ethic they found in their employees: "They don't want to lead, they don't want to follow. They want interesting work and satisfying emotional relationships, characterized by 'kindness, sympathy, understanding,' and 'generosity.'"[4]

Here's an interesting paradox. The more our culture has moved away from a biblical perspective of work, the less satisfied we have become with our work. Yet, at the same time, we have become more obsessive about our work, as evidenced by the number of stress-related illnesses. Even Christians have allowed their attitudes about their work—in the workplace, school, or work inside the home—to be shaped by culture rather than God's Word.

Three different views about work are commonly held by Christians today:

WORK AS OUR GOD

Those who hold this secular philosophy of life contend that we will find our meaning and purpose in life through our work, not through a relationship with God. Such people derive their identity from what they do instead of from who they are. For example, the next time you are in a group in which everyone introduces himself, notice how many people give their vocation right after their name.

This excessive emphasis on vocation spills over into our parenting. When our children reach a certain age, we begin wondering what they will "do" with their lives. We communicate the idea that the focal point of their lives will be their vocation. Often we spend more time worrying about what they will do in life, rather than what kind of person they will become.

Men are especially prone to the worship of work. Recently, I had lunch with a very successful banker and his wife. A few years before, the banker suffered a serious heart attack. His doctors told him he would have to either moderate his exhausting work schedule or risk losing his life. The warning was enough to get his attention—for a while. But he confessed to me that a year later he was right back to a twelve-hours-a-day, six-days-a-week work schedule. As he related to me the details of his job, his wife said, "You can tell he loves his work, can't you?" He didn't just love his work—he worshiped it!

But is our work really deserving of such a prominent place in our hearts? Solomon explained the consequences of worshiping our work:

> Thus I hated all the fruit of my labor for which I had labored under the sun, for I must leave it to the man who will come after me. And who knows whether he will be a wise man or a fool? Yet he will have control over all the fruit of my labor for which I have labored by acting wisely under the sun. (Eccles. 2:18-19)

Why pour your energy into something that you ultimately will leave to someone who may or may not be a good steward of your estate? Perhaps Solomon was writing from his own experience. Remember that King Solomon turned over the leadership reins of Israel to his son Rehoboam. In less than a year, Rehoboam's lack of wisdom caused the great nation to be torn apart by civil war. Solomon says it is futile to center your life around things you will leave to someone else.

A few months before my father died of cancer, he was spending his time making sure his business affairs were in order. I will never forget sitting with him at our kitchen table listening to him detail for me the location of his bank accounts, stock certificates, gold coins, and other assets so that I could settle the estate when he would die within a few weeks. Suddenly he stopped, looked at me, and said partly in jest, but partly in truth, "I can't believe I am getting ready to leave everything I have spent my life working for to someone else to enjoy!" That is the wisdom that only death brings.

However, whether your successor manages or squanders

your life's work will make no difference to you anyway, because you will be gone! Jesus taught this same truth in the story about the rich fool. A man spent every waking moment thinking about his work. Even at night, he could not sleep, because he was so consumed with accumulating more. But in the middle of one of those sleepless nights, God came to him and said, "You fool! This very night your soul is required of you; and now who will own what you have prepared?" Jesus concluded, "So is the man who lays up treasure for himself, and is not rich toward God" (Luke 12:20-21).

The transitory nature of life makes the worship of our work a poor choice. We Christians, who understand that truth, may allow that understanding to lead us to another extreme attitude about work.

WORK AS OUR JUDGMENT
Some Christians have so reacted to the worship of work in our society that they have labeled work as a necessary evil. Those who accept this view even use Scripture to support their idea. They point to Genesis 3:17-19:

> Cursed is the ground because of you; in toil you shall eat of it all the days of your life. Both thorns and thistles it shall grow for you; and you shall eat the plants of the field; by the sweat of your face you shall eat bread, till you return to the ground.

According to this view, which had its origins in the Middle Ages, all of life can be categorized as either "sacred" or "secular." Everything that took place within the church was "sacred"; everything outside the church was "secular." This philosophy is built upon the very unbiblical idea that places "the soul over the body, the eternal over the temporal, and the clergy over the laity."[5]

If all work can be classified as either sacred or secular and if only what happens in the church is sacred, the conclusion is very simple. Christians should quit their jobs, enroll in the seminary, and all become pastors, missionaries, or other vocational Christian servants. In fact, that is what happened in early church history as believers left their vocations and headed for the monastery.

The same phenomenon is appearing today. An increasing number of thirty-six- to forty-five-year-old people are giving up promising careers to attend a theological seminary. Some have definite ministry goals in mind; others are not sure why they want to attend, but they have the nagging feeling that there must be more in life. I think I understand why.

After constantly being told that only those things that "count for eternity" are worthwhile, some Christians become understandably discontented with their jobs. After all, if I'm an engineer, a secretary, or a vacuum cleaner salesman, I have a difficult time seeing how what I do is going to make any eternal difference. I may have occasional opportunities to share my faith with a coworker, but not many. Therefore, my work, which accounts for 70 percent of my life, is worthless and meaningless to God.

But this assumed dichotomy between sacred and secular is flawed. First of all, the distinction between the present and eternity is a false one. We should rethink what we mean when we emphasize "things that count for eternity." I believe we make a mistake to define "eternity" as beginning beyond the grave. Instead, we should see eternity as something apart from time—no beginning and no end—an unbroken, continuing line. Only a portion of the line, our life span, is visible to us; yet it is still connected to the unseen endless portion. What we do on this side of the grave is just as important to God as what happens on the other side of the grave.

And that leads to a second flaw in this viewpoint. We need a broader concept of God's "work." God's work extends beyond evangelism and discipleship. The Bible clearly states that we can glorify God now by whatever task we perform—inside or outside the four walls of the church. "And whatever you do in word or deed, do all in the name of the Lord Jesus, giving thanks through Him to God the Father. . . . Whatever you do, do your work heartily, as for the Lord rather than for men" (Col. 3:17, 23). A. W. Tozer commented: "It is not what a man does that determines whether his work is sacred or secular, but why he does it." We will discuss this idea further when we look at "Keys to Guilt-Free Work."

WORK AS A PLATFORM

In their book *Your Work Matters to God*, Doug Sherman and William Hendricks mention a third view that some Christians have adopted about their work: work as a soapbox. Taking seriously the great commission to evangelize the world, yet realizing the impracticality of every Christian quitting his secular vocation to enter the ministry (after all, who would pay all of these new ministers?), this view of work says the following: "My work is of value to the extent that it provides opportunities for ministry." Thus, work is still viewed as a necessary evil—but an evil that can be partially redeemed. To the extent that my job allows me to witness for Christ, provides me with paid vacation time to go on mission trips, or at least provides income that I can give to Christian causes, my work is important.

This view of a Christian's work has some merit but is still flawed. It is true that we should seize every opportunity to be a witness for Christ. And our income from our secular jobs should be used to support the work of God's kingdom. But this view, like the "work as a curse" model, still undervalues the importance of work.

According to the biblical model, your job—whatever it is—has value in itself. Every job is a sacred calling from God that is used to further his kingdom's work. And while God's kingdom's work certainly includes evangelism and discipleship, it is not limited to these ministries.

THE BIBLICAL VIEW OF WORK

How do I know that work—whatever it is—has value to God? First of all, God created man to work. Have you ever wondered why God made us? Your first answer might be "to have fellowship with him." Yet, when we turn to the creation account in Genesis 1, we find something completely different. God articulates his "purpose statement" for man very clearly:

> Then God said, "Let Us make man in Our image, according to Our likeness; and let them *rule* over the fish of the sea and over the birds of the sky and over the cattle and over all the earth, and over every creeping thing that creeps on the earth. . . . And God blessed them; and God said to them, "Be fruitful and multiply, and fill the earth, and *subdue* it; and *rule* over the fish of the sea and over the birds of the sky, and over every living thing that moves on the earth." (1:26, 28, emphasis mine)

God created man to work! And the work described here is not limited to the "spiritual." The original work God envisioned for man had nothing to do with evangelism or discipleship. The work God created for man was very practical—caring for the animals and farming the land. By the way, notice that these verses were written *before* the Fall in Genesis 3.

To view our work as a curse from God is totally unbiblical. Yes, work has been made harder because of the Fall. Wrong motives, strained relationships, slothfulness, physical limitations, and sexual temptation are common problems we all encounter in the workplace. Nevertheless, work itself is a gift from God, as Solomon observed:

> There is nothing better for a man than to eat and drink and tell himself that his labor is good. This also I have seen, that it is from the hand of God. For who can eat and who can have enjoyment without Him? (Eccles. 2:24-25)

The creation account also teaches us another truth about work: Our work is an extension of God's work: "And the Lord God planted a garden toward the east, in Eden; and there He placed the man whom He had formed. . . . Then the Lord God took the man and put him into the garden of Eden to cultivate it and keep it" (Gen. 2:8, 15).

Now, think with me for just a moment. The setting is the beautiful Garden of Eden. The time is before the Fall and its resulting curse on the ground. Yet God created the world in such a way that it was not self-sustaining. It still needed cultivating and preserving. And God created man to fulfill that task. It is not as if God *needed* Adam. God is self-sufficient. He could have made the earth in such a way that it needed no human intervention. Yet God chose to design the universe in such a way that makes our work an extension of his work.[6]

Perhaps you have heard the story about the farmer who purchased an old, run-down piece of property. The ground was completely overtaken with weeds, the equipment was rusting, the farmhouse was falling down. The farmer spent months cultivating the land, purchasing new equipment, painting and repairing the farmhouse. One day the preacher pulled up while the man was out working in the hot sun. "You and God have done a marvelous job with this place," the preacher said. The farmer, wiping the sweat from his brow, said, "You should have seen this place when God had it all to himself!"

Such an attitude might seem cocky and prideful to us, but it is actually biblical. Our work is a partnership with God. God and Adam were in business together. As Augustine said, "Without God, we can not. Without us, God will not."

Let's review what we have seen so far:

1. Our culture has moved farther and farther away from the biblical view of work, resulting in Americans working harder and enjoying it less.
2. Our ideas of work have shifted gradually throughout history. Every age has in some way distorted the biblical model for work; yet all of these distortions share the idea that work is not a sacred calling but an opportunity for personal fulfillment.
3. This ever-changing attitude about work has also caused Christians to go to one of two extremes about their work. Either they tend to worship their work, looking to their jobs to give them ultimate satisfaction, or they tend to despise their work, seeing it as a necessary evil in a fallen world.
4. The Bible views all work as a sacred calling. Man, created in God's image, was destined to be a worker. Man's work is an extension of the Creator's continuing work.

After seeing what the Bible says about work, how do you feel about *your* work? The thesis of this book is that God wants us to experience closure—satisfaction—in each area of life.

Do you look forward to getting out of bed Monday morning to face a new week on the job? Do you believe that part of God's sovereign plan for your life includes your vocation? Is your identity in life basically tied to your profession (how would your feelings about yourself change if you were no longer to perform the job you now hold)? Is your life properly balanced between work, leisure, family, and spiritual pursuits? Do you find yourself continually thinking about your job?

Your answers to those questions will help you determine whether you are really experiencing closure in your work. If you find yourself depressed by your job, or if you are obsessed by your work, you are not experiencing the kind of closure God wants you to have. Whether you are a homemaker, a student, a vocational Christian worker, or a corporate executive, certain important principles will help you to enjoy guilt-free work.

KEYS TO EXPERIENCING GUILT-FREE WORK

1. Gain God's perspective about work.

It is important that we guard against the cultural distortions about work. As we saw earlier, secularists tend to overemphasize the importance of our jobs, turning them into all-consuming idols that demand our total allegiance. On the other hand, some Christians tend to underemphasize the importance of work, viewing it as a curse that prohibits them from concentrating on "eternal things."

The truth is that our work—whatever it is—is an opportunity for us to glorify God by working in partnership with him. As long as our job is not illegal, immoral, or in some way in opposition to God's purpose, our work is contributing to God's kingdom.

The problem is that many Christians have limited God's work to the areas of evangelism or discipleship. If our work does not directly contribute to those two goals, we tend to view our work as secular. But I believe God's purpose extends beyond evangelism and discipleship.

For example, is God interested in justice? Of course he is. The Old Testament prophets were continually chastising the Israelites for injustice. Remember Micah 6:8: "And what does the Lord require of you but to do justice, to love kindness, and to walk humbly with your God?" If you are involved in law enforcement or the judicial system, you are part of God's kingdom's work.

Does God's purpose include providing for the needs of his children? Of course it does! What do we need? At the very least we need food, clothing, and housing. Then farming, ranching, textiles, construction, and hundreds of related industries are a part of God's kingdom's work.

Money magazine carried an article several years ago about a Christian who found a unique way to use his work to provide for the needs of God's children. Thirty-eight-year-old R. Theodore Benna had been a consultant with the Philadelphia employee-benefits firm, Johnson Cos., for fifteen years. Yet his job left him unfulfilled. Benna was a devout Christian who wanted to do something unique with his life. He says that through prayer, God opened his eyes to a little-known provision in the Internal Revenue Service Code, section 401(k), that would allow employees to defer some of their income into a retirement plan and would also allow employers to contribute to that plan. He designed such a program for his own company and used it as a test case with the IRS. That was more than twenty years ago. Today, millions of workers will enjoy a secure retirement through a 401(k) retirement plan. Why? Because Mr. Benna asked God to use his profession to serve a greater purpose. And God chose to use Mr. Benna's plan to provide for the needs of his children.[7]

We make a great mistake when we draw a false dichotomy between "secular" and "sacred" work. God's kingdom is bigger than that. An epitaph on a tombstone in London reads: "To Thomas Cobb who mended shoes in this village for forty years *to the glory of God*" (emphasis mine).[8]

Your work, whatever it is, is a divine assignment from God.

2. Understand your responsibilities in your work.

The way to experience closure in any area of life is to first understand God's requirements. What does God require of our work? In Colossians 3:23–4:1, the apostle Paul outlined two guidelines for a Christian's work:

1. OUR WORK IS TO BE CHARACTERIZED BY QUALITY.

Author John Gardner, in his book *Excellence*, said, "We must have excellent plumbers as well as philosophers, otherwise neither our pipes nor our philosophies will hold water."[9] After years of being savaged by the Japanese, our automobile manufacturers as well as other industries are understanding the importance of excellence. There are certainly some practical reasons for producing quality work.

But the apostle Paul gives us an even higher motivation for excellence than the profit motive:

> Whatever you do, do your work heartily, as for the Lord rather than for men; knowing that from the Lord you will receive the reward of the inheritance. It is the Lord Christ whom you serve. (Col. 3:23-24)

Paul wrote that ultimate rewards, or lack of reward, will come from God himself.

2. OUR WORK IS TO BE CHARACTERIZED BY INTEGRITY. In this same passage Paul encourages us to be ethical in our work: "For he who does wrong will receive the consequences of the

wrong which he has done, and that without partiality" (Col. 3:25).

If indeed the Lord is going to judge our work, we need to be careful that we maintain Christian principles in our work. Certainly a whole book could be devoted to ethics in the workplace.

Paul warned employees not to steal from their employer. That is the wrong Paul has in mind here. How do I know? In the Colossian church there was a slave owner named Philemon. One of Philemon's slaves, Onesimus, had stolen from Philemon and had run away. When Onesimus came to Rome, he met Paul and was converted. Paul urged Onesimus to return home and to return the stolen goods. (The New Testament letter Philemon is Paul's appeal to this slave owner to treat his repentant slave with compassion.)

In Colossians 3 Paul commanded all other slaves in Colossae not to repeat the mistake of Onesimus. Although you might never consider dipping into the cash register at work, there are many ways to steal from your employer. You can rob your employer of time by coming to work late, leaving early, or not giving a full day's labor for your pay. You can rob him of reputation by slandering him or the company outside the office. You can rob him of property by taking things from the office that do not belong to you—money, equipment, postage, or office supplies.

McKenna illustrates the practical results of honesty in the workplace:

> The founder of a national insurance corporation believed that honesty extended to paper clips. He tells about an up and coming executive who was on the fast track to becoming president. However, when the chairman discovered that this young executive kept his office at home stocked

with office paper clips, he fired him. In an act of retribution, the executive set up a rival insurance company that ended up in bankruptcy. It was later discovered that this executive had falsified records to begin his new company. Every year at the annual orientation for new employees, the chairman of the first company began by saying, "Honesty begins with paper clips."[10]

Paul also addressed the employer's responsibilities to his employees. "Masters, grant to your slaves justice and fairness, knowing that you too have a Master in heaven" (Col 4:1). Employers are to show the same compassion for their workers that God shows for us. An employer should clearly spell out his expectations to the employee, be compassionate, and deal with his employees justly. That means that he is to compensate them fairly, that he is not to exploit them, and that he is to avoid favoritism. The employer is to be a model of how God deals with his children.

God's requirements for our work are not extensive, but they are precise. God requires that we strive for quality in what we do while we maintain ethical standards in our dealings with others.

3. Avoid obsession with your work.

Since work is a divine assignment from God, he has some standards for our work. But we need to keep our work in balance with other areas. Our work is only one aspect of our life and our relationship with God. Just as our life consists of more than our possessions, life consists of more than our work.

How can you tell if you are becoming obsessive about your work? In her book *Working Ourselves to Death*, Dr. Diane Fassel discusses the progression of workaholism.

The Work Addiction Scale

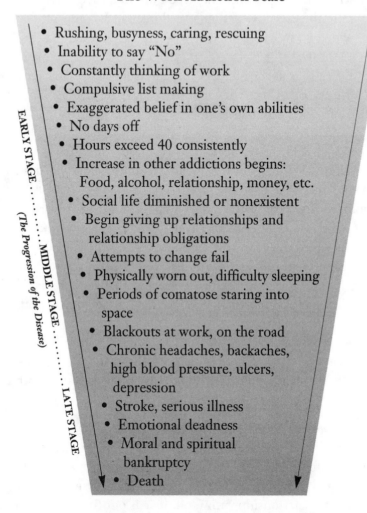

EARLY STAGE .... MIDDLE STAGE .... LATE STAGE
(The Progression of the Disease)

- Rushing, busyness, caring, rescuing
- Inability to say "No"
- Constantly thinking of work
- Compulsive list making
- Exaggerated belief in one's own abilities
- No days off
- Hours exceed 40 consistently
- Increase in other addictions begins:
  Food, alcohol, relationship, money, etc.
- Social life diminished or nonexistent
- Begin giving up relationships and
  relationship obligations
- Attempts to change fail
- Physically worn out, difficulty sleeping
- Periods of comatose staring into
  space
- Blackouts at work, on the road
- Chronic headaches, backaches,
  high blood pressure, ulcers,
  depression
- Stroke, serious illness
- Emotional deadness
- Moral and spiritual
  bankruptcy
- Death

Dr. Fassel concludes by saying, "Healthy people are enlivened and stimulated by work. They don't expect work to make them whole. They are whole and they choose to work. Sure, such people are tired at the end of a day, but not with the disabling exhaustion of the work addict."[11]

4. Experience closure on a regular basis.

By this I mean that we need to build relaxation into a regular schedule. Such relaxation is vital to our physical, emotional, and spiritual health. Those people are mistaken who think that they must keep working sixteen hours a day, seven days a week to get ahead. Such workaholism is not a requirement for success.

Albert Einstein is an example of a man who changed the course of science and history without working like a dog. Einstein worked in his lab in the morning. He spent his afternoons sailing. He came upon the theory of relativity when "One day while I was eating an apple, the answer appeared to me and said, 'Here I am.'"[12]

God taught us the principle of saying "enough" in the fourth commandment:

> Six days you shall labor and do all your work, but the seventh day is a sabbath of the Lord your God; in it you shall not do any work, you or your son or your daughter, your male or your female servant or your cattle or your sojourner who stays with you. For in six days the Lord made the heavens and the earth, the sea and all that is in them, and rested on the seventh day; therefore the Lord blessed the sabbath day and made it holy. (Exod. 20:9-11)

Part of God's plan for our work is that we enjoy a minivacation once a week. His command that we cease from labor (that is the literal meaning of *sabbath*—to stop from doing) was for *our* benefit, not God's. More will be said about relaxation in the next chapter.

God wants us to do more than endure our work. He wants us to enjoy it. But enjoyment will only occur when we gain God's perspective about our work. Such a perspective involves seeing our work as a divine assignment from God that has meaning and value. But such a perspective also recognizes that our work is only one facet of our relationship with God.

All of this discussion about work is making me tired! So let's take a few minutes and see what God has to say about the flip side of work—relaxation. I guarantee it will surprise you.

CHAPTER 5

. . . . .

Guilt-Free
Relaxation

HOW are you at wasting time? At first, you might say you are an expert. "Procrastination is my spiritual gift!" But by wasting time, I am not referring to procrastination, but to the ability to relax. Are you able to spend hours at a time without working, or even *thinking* about work?

If someone were to give you an entire day to do anything you wanted with one restriction—no work could be involved— would you be elated or frustrated? Suppose that gift were to come once a week? I realize that some of you would have no problem with such a gift. If that is the case, you might want to skip this chapter or (better yet) read it through the eyes of someone you know who has trouble relaxing.

But I believe that many of you (like myself) may wrestle with the ability to enjoy guilt-free relaxation. It is not that you don't enjoy a day at the beach, or an afternoon spent window-shopping at the mall, or sleeping in on your day off. But during such periods of relaxation, a small voice inside you reminds you that you really should be doing something else. You can't forget the project at work that is due next week, the repairs that need to be made around the house, or the letter that begs to be answered. Such tasks rob you of your ability to enjoy guilt-free relaxation.

I am reminded of this problem every time our family takes a vacation. Although I know intellectually that I need a vacation, and even though my church gives me a generous amount of time off every year, I have difficulty spending a week "doing nothing." As we prepared to go to Colorado last summer, I found myself packing all kinds of books that I wanted to read in order to "get ahead" for the coming year. Every afternoon at the pool, I brought a legal pad on which I listed all of the tasks that needed to be performed when I returned. And one afternoon I decided it would be advantageous to schedule a business appointment at a nearby Christian organization since "I was already there." The result? Most of the books never got read, and many of my lists were incomplete. All I really accomplished was to rob myself of the opportunity to unwind. Instead of returning back to work invigorated and ready for the coming year, I came back from my "vacation" just as tired as when I left. In fact, the first few weeks back on the job were extremely unproductive.

My vacation scenario is not unique to me. The wife of a successful businessman in our church complained to me that her husband insisted on taking his fax machine with him on their vacation so that he could keep in touch with the office. He spent their week at the beach constantly hovering over that machine, waiting for any "news."

And that leads me to the thesis of this chapter. Those who fail to learn the importance of guilt-free relaxation will constantly find themselves working at their play and playing at their work. Relaxation is not an option but an *essential* for experiencing a satisfying and productive life.

In the last two chapters we have touched on the subject of relaxation as it relates to time management and work. But in this chapter we are going to look at the issue in depth.

Walter Kerr may be describing your life when he writes:

> I'm going to start out by assuming that you are approximately as unhappy as I am. Neither of us may be submitting ourselves to psychiatrists, neither of us may take an excessive number of tranquilizers each day, neither of us may have married three times in an effort to find someone to make us happier. We are not (quite yet) desperate, but we are, vaguely, dissatisfied. . . . We are vaguely wretched because we are living half lives, half-heartedly, and with only one half of our minds actively engaged in making contact with the universe around us.[1]

Does that describe you? If so, your dissatisfaction with life may be due to your inability to enjoy guilt-free relaxation.

WHY DON'T WE RELAX?

It is a paradox that Americans are enjoying more leisure time each year and yet having such a difficult time relaxing. I see at least six reasons why people refuse to build periods of relaxation into their schedules.

1. Failure to understand the importance of relaxation

Think for a moment about how a rubber band can be stretched and then the tension relaxed briefly. The process can be continued indefinitely without destroying the rubber band. But stretch it too far, or keep it stretched for a long period of time, and it will snap.

The same is true about stress in our lives. Stress is the price we pay for living. We experience all kinds of it on a regular basis: financial concerns, relationship pressures, and the minor irritations of daily life such as stopped-up plumbing, cars needing repair, standing behind someone with twenty items in the express lane of the supermarket. Stress in and of itself is not necessarily bad. In fact, some stress can actually be productive. James, the half brother of Jesus, wrote, "Consider it all joy, my brethren, when you encounter various trials, knowing that the testing of your faith produces endurance" (James 1:2-3).

In the world of mechanics, stress can strengthen some metals. But if the pressure is too great, the metal fails. The same is true in our lives. Dr. John Morely, professor of geriatrics at the St. Louis University School of Medicine, wrote that some stress in our lives is good for us. He says that both physical and mental stress are directly responsible for the release of beta-endorphin, which strengthens special cells in our body that reduce the growth of cancerous tumors. But such stress must be kept under control. Dr. Morely says, "The stress that you adequately cope with may be good for you, whereas stress that you fail to cope with . . . is most probably bad for you. Short bursts of stress are OK. Long bursts could be a problem."[2]

What kinds of physical problems can prolonged stress induce? Research is now showing a link between stress, high cholesterol, and cancer:

> Until the 1980s, most physicians associated abnormally high levels of cholesterol solely with diet. More recent research, however, has established a connection between emotional stress or physical fatigue and abnormally high cholesterol. . . . High cholesterol levels have been found in accountants approaching IRS deadlines, or in medical students approaching examinations. High cholesterol counts, whether from food or emotional stress, can represent an invitation to heart attacks, but, as Dr. Goad and his

associates have found, they can be a portal for a wide range of other illnesses as well, since a heavy burden of fat can do damage to the immune system.[3]

Like the rubber band, we need to learn to relax the tension in our lives or suffer the physical, as well as emotional and spiritual, results.

2. Belief that relaxation is "unproductive"

Some of us are infected with a disease that appears harmless but that is progressively destroying us: workaholism. If you suffer from this disease, you already know some of the symptoms (for a more complete list, see the chart in the last chapter):

- Your workweek continually exceeds forty hours.
- You are constantly checking in with the office on your day off or while on vacation.
- Your conversation with friends centers around your job.
- You experience difficulty sleeping at night.

Dr. Diane Fassel has described workaholism as a "killer stalking our society." John O. Neikirk calls it "the pain others applaud." Bryan Robinson calls it "the only lifeboat guaranteed to sink." Fassel goes on to write that workaholism is the "cleanest of all addictions" because it seems to be productive.[4] Those who work sixty to seventy hours a week are more productive than those who don't. Right? Wrong.

Not only does workaholism rob us of relaxation; it also impairs our ability to perform productively. Those who refuse to balance their lives with regular periods of relaxation will find themselves making mistakes at work that take even more time to correct. Their ability to concentrate on the work will diminish. And they will find themselves increasingly daydreaming while on the job.

When Tim Hansel wrote his wonderful book *When I Relax I Feel Guilty*, he expressed the feeling of many Christians. I have always thought the title of that book was most interesting. Notice that the title is not *If I Relax I Feel Guilty*, but **When I Relax**. . . . The issue is not whether you will relax, but when. Whether you realize it or not, your body *is* going to relax. It has to relax in order to survive.

3. Lack of proper self-esteem

Those who have difficulty relaxing many times either underestimate or overestimate their own abilities. Let me explain. People who suffer from poor self-esteem tend to derive their sense of personal worth from their work. Feeling that they have no inherent value in who they are as people, they find their significance through increased activity. They conclude that the more they accomplish, the more worthy they are as individuals.

The doctor who works one hundred hours a week usually does not do so out of financial necessity; instead, he may be trying to compensate for a lack of self-worth he has carried with him since childhood. A recently promoted executive may find herself working unusually long hours out of an irrational fear of failure. She secretly feels unqualified for the job and feels she must ensure her success. Again, an issue of poor self-esteem.

How does this affect the issue of relaxation? A person with poor self-esteem who is trying to define his worth as a human being through his work cannot afford to relax. To quit working increases the risk of failure or insignificance—two possibilities this person cannot handle.

I recently read a story that perfectly describes the plight of the workaholic:

A TRUE STORY

One day in late 1969, in the research library of the University of California at Berkeley, a young man went berserk. He ran through the library, shouting hysterically at his astonished fellow students, "Stop! Stop! You're getting ahead of me!"

He was arrested. But what was his crime, really? Being in the wrong decade. As we all know, the sixties era and its childish preoccupation with peace, good sex, and battered VW buses, was little more than a black mark, a shameful demerit in the History of Stress.

Now, of course, in the stress-filled eighties, this concept of "getting ahead of me" has regained its rightful place of importance. In fact, it is one of the basic precepts of stress.

Simply stated, people are getting ahead of you. All the time.

While you're at your desk, people working out at the gym are getting ahead of you.

While you're at the gym, your coworkers are getting ahead of you.

If a friend gets a promotion at work, she has gotten ahead of you.

If a colleague reads a book you haven't read, he has gotten ahead of you.

The entire U.S. swim team has gotten ahead of you.

While you're reading this book, everyone is getting ahead of you.

The beauty of this concept is that it can be applied across the board, anywhere, anytime.

On the road? Drivers of more expensive cars have gotten ahead of you.

Watching TV? All the writers, actors, and technical crews have gotten ahead of you.

At Marine World? The dolphins have gotten ahead of you.

Always judge yourself, and your intrinsic moral worth, in terms of specific achievements as compared to others.

Always judge any situation in relation to how much the people involved have gotten ahead of you, and in what ways.[5]

That is the dilemma of the person with low self-esteem.

Yet the person who overestimates his own importance also has difficulty relaxing. The life motto of this person is If it's going to be, it's up to me! He or she usually overestimates the number of projects that can be done well. Lesser mortals require food and rest—but not this person, who is "different" (translation: superior). Tasks cannot be delegated, because no one else is as capable of doing the job as well. This person cannot afford to relax. Why? To do so risks the collapse of the entire organization.

If you sense a little passion in my words, it is because the disgusting person I am describing in the above paragraph is me. Leaders can easily overestimate their own importance in an organization, because they feel so much pressure for its success.

I love the story about the preacher who checked out of his office every afternoon at 3:00 P.M. to go down to the railroad tracks and watch the train roll through town. After several months his deacons pulled him aside and questioned him about this strange habit. Why was he so fascinated with the train? "Because it is the only thing in town I don't have to push!"

I used to have more of a problem with this issue. I spent seven years at my former church running at a frantic pace. The church was in the process of dying when I came. But after seven years the attendance doubled in size, and I was called to another church. Many people wondered what would happen when

"Brother Robert" left. Surely, some thought, the church would collapse. Guess what? The church went eight months without a pastor, and during that time the church *grew!* Just to goad me a little, my former members would send me charts comparing attendance figures to the time I had been there! Now the church has called a pastor who is much more laid back than I could ever be, and the church continues to prosper. So much for my importance!

God does not want us to either underestimate or overestimate our importance. Every Christian has unique strengths as well as weaknesses. We should thank God for our gifts and depend on others to complement our weaknesses. The apostle Paul advised:

> For by the grace given me I say to every one of you: Do not think of yourself more highly than you ought, but rather think of yourself with sober judgment, in accordance with the measure of faith God has given you. Just as each of us has one body with many members, and these members do not all have the same function, so in Christ we who are many form one body, and each member belongs to all the others. We have different gifts, according to the grace given us. (Rom. 12:3-6, NIV)

4. Materialism

Another barrier to relaxation is materialism. The desire for more fuels some people's obsession with their work. For them relaxation translates into unearned income. An increasing stream of income is essential to maintain the lifestyle to which they have become accustomed. The result is that some people feel they cannot afford to relax. In his book *Men in Midlife Crisis*, Jim Conway describes a man caught in this dilemma:

If it weren't for his massive domestic responsibilities, he'd give up his job immediately. He's hated it for years anyway, but it provides the $70,000 a year he needs for his house, three cars, and cottage on the lake, not to mention keeping the kids in college and taking vacations to various parts of the world. If he didn't have all of these family responsibilities, he could give up his job and do something more simple.[6]

Bill is a successful architect in our church. Yet his philosophy of work defies the current models of success. Bill refuses to work more than forty hours a week, even though his services are in such demand that he could easily bill one hundred hours a week. No, Bill is not lazy. But an unexpected event convinced him of the importance of a well-balanced life.

When he started out in the business over a decade ago, he was working around the clock. He enjoyed his job and was making a wonderful income. The only problem was that he never saw his family. Nevertheless, he had a beautiful home and a growing bank account.

Then one day a tornado came to visit our city. Hiding under a kitchen table one afternoon, he watched in horror as the wind ripped his house apart and threatened to destroy his family. It was at that moment that he saw life as it really is: brief and fragile. Bill made a commitment at that point. If God allowed him and his family to survive that ordeal, he would make them, not his work, his priority. Today Bill still enjoys his work. But he realizes there is more to life than work and the accumulation of assets that can be so easily lost.

Bill is not unique. A growing number of Americans are refusing to allow materialism to rob them of a full and balanced life. James D. Schwartz cites the following examples:

A headline from the August 8, 1989, issue of *Fortune* magazine asked, "Is Greed Dead?" It cited a poll stating that 75 percent of twenty-five- to forty-nine-year-old Americans said they'd like to see this country return to a "simpler lifestyle" with less emphasis on material success.

Time magazine's cover story on April 9, 1991, titled "The Simple Life: Rejecting the Rat Race. Americans Get Back to Basics" recorded Dan Rather's September 11 CBS newscast. The article concluded that "upscale is out; downscale is in. . . . In place of materialism, many Americans are . . . thinking hard about what really matters in their lives, and they've decided to make some changes."

In 1990, a real estate agent told author Richard Reeves in *Money* magazine that he could afford a bigger house in a better neighborhood if he wanted it. However, he had decided to use their extra money to travel and relax. As he said, "I have discovered that there really is such a thing as "enough.""[7]

Not knowing how to say "enough" is a formidable barrier to enjoying guilt-free relaxation.

5. Poor work habits

Some people's guilt about relaxation can be traced to poor work habits. The scenario goes something like this. Instead of working hard while "on the clock," a person spends a large amount of his work time in nonproductive activities: longer-than-average lunches, talking with coworkers, extended telephone conversations, and so on. When the end of the workweek rolls around, this individual finds himself exhausted, even though he has accomplished little. The result of his slothfulness is that he is always under the gun about approaching or missed deadlines.

On the other hand, he cannot truly enjoy his time off because

(a) deep down he knows he does not deserve it and/or (b) he is filled with fear that his slothfulness will be exposed, and he will lose his job. Thus, this person will always find himself playing at his work and working at his play.

The solution to such a dilemma is to learn to be more productive at work so that you can enjoy guilt-free relaxation. In his book *The Time Crunch*, Greg Asimakoupoulos quotes a CEO as saying the major culprit of lack of productivity in corporations is a lack of self-discipline. "All you need is a big pot of glue. You smear some on your chair and some on the seat of your pants. You sit down and you stick with every project until you've done the best you can."[8]

Some of you may wonder how that philosophy fits in with the theme of this chapter. But I am convinced one reason we may have difficulty relaxing is because we don't feel we deserve to—a feeling that is sometimes justified.

6. Failure to understand the biblical mandate to relax

To enjoy a guilt-free life we must understand God's requirements and reject unrealistic expectations that we or others generate for ourselves. What does God's Word say about this issue of relaxation? More than you might think. God did not create us to work seven days a week. To do so is to violate his plan for our lives.

As we saw in chapter 4, God has designed a work/relaxation rhythm. We work six days and relax one day. That one day of relaxation is called the Sabbath. The word *Sabbath* comes from the Hebrew word *shabbath*, which means "to stop, to desist, to cease from doing." Dietrich Bonhoeffer suggests that the word means "to rest from even the thought of labor!" God commands that one day a week we refuse to work.

This concept of the Sabbath is so important that God devotes more space to it than any other of the Ten Commandments.

Unfortunately, many Christians have reduced and twisted the idea of the Sabbath into a list of restrictions of what we cannot do on this day of rest. The Pharisees made the same mistake. They were continually haranguing Jesus about his observance of the Sabbath. But Jesus made it very clear that the Sabbath was for our benefit. God gave us the Sabbath as a gift: "The Sabbath was made for man, and not man for the Sabbath" (Mark 2:27).

A Sabbath day is crucial for our physical well-being. We are not designed to work seven days a week. God told us three thousand years ago what doctors and production analysts are telling us today: Work without rest can cause serious illness as well as a decrease in productivity. Workaholics top the charts in work-related disorders such as high blood pressure and premature heart attacks. God knew this all along, so he designed a mini-vacation for us every week. It's called the Sabbath.

Sabbath rest is also necessary for our emotional well-being. Many times the emotional stress of work is more damaging than the physical stress.

William Wilberforce was a member of the English Parliament in the early 1800s. Wilberforce, a committed Christian, was responsible for leading the passage of legislation that abolished slavery in the British Empire. But Wilberforce had a problem with ambition. His biographer notes that rising ambition would have destroyed Wilberforce had it not been for his strict observance of Sunday as a Sabbath. On Sundays, he refused to work or even think about work. In his spiritual journal, Wilberforce wrote, "Blessed be to God for the day of rest and religious occupation wherein earthly things assume their true size. Ambition is stunted."[9]

During that time two of Wilberforce's friends committed suicide. About them he wrote, "With peaceful Sundays, the strings would never have snapped as they did from over tension."[10]

Sabbaths are a time to loosen the strings. Such days remind us that there is more to life than work. I have always been fascinated by Exodus 31:17: "For in six days the Lord made heaven and earth, but on the seventh day He ceased from labor, and *was refreshed!*" (emphasis mine). If God the Father, the omnipotent Creator of the universe, could be refreshed by a Sabbath day, how much more do we need it!

How to Enjoy Guilt-Free Relaxation

As you can see, God's Word not only permits but prescribes regular periods of relaxation. How can you enjoy those times of relaxation to the fullest?

In the above section, we discussed some barriers to guilt-free relaxation. As we remove the barriers of poor self-esteem, materialism, poor work habits, and a lack of understanding about God's view of rest, we are already on the road to learning how to relax. Let me suggest several other steps that will help you in balancing work and rest:

1. Learn to handle worry.

It's confession time. I worry a lot. I know that "men of the cloth" are not supposed to worry, but I do. And the times I am most prone to worry are those times when I am not working and my mind is free to wander. Friday nights are the worst for me. After a long week, I look forward to taking my wife out to dinner, then coming home and reading or watching a news program on television. It is during those relaxed times that I begin to worry about the stock market, my family's physical safety, the church, my health, people I may have offended during the week—you name it, I have worried about it.

Several years ago my wife and I took a trip to New York for

a week of vacation. On the plane I read a magazine article about the possible insolvency of the Federal Deposit Insurance Corporation and the resulting collapse of the banking industry. I got so worked up over the article that I spent much of our vacation on the phone to my banker friend in Dallas and my bank in Massachusetts, checking their balance sheet! (You can tell by this time that I have a difficult time with vacations.)

I doubt I am the only one with this problem. Worry is an effective saboteur of guilt-free relaxation. That is why it is so important that we learn to handle anxiety. I believe that there are at least three sources of anxiety in our lives. Determining the source of our fears is an important step in removing them and experiencing the kind of rest God wants us to enjoy.

Sometimes worry is *a symptom of unconfessed sin* in our life. David spent six months worrying that his hidden sin with Bathsheba would be exposed: "When I kept silent about my sin, my body wasted away through my groaning all day long. For day and night Thy hand was heavy upon me; my vitality was drained away as with the fever heat of summer" (Ps. 32:3-4). As in David's case, worry can be a warning signal of something wrong in our relationship with God.

The remedy for this type of anxiety is to acknowledge our sin and turn from it. That is what David finally did. Once he confessed his sin and turned from it, he once again experienced joy in his life (Ps. 51:12).

Many times worry is *a tool used by Satan* to paralyze and neutralize God's people. Such anxiety, often having no logical basis, is a direct attack of the enemy. Dr. Walter Cavert, in his study of anxiety, concluded that only 8 percent of people's worries were legitimate. In other words, 92 percent of what we worry about has no foundation.[11]

Isn't that just like the devil? Jesus reminded us that Satan is the father of all lies (John 8:44), and lies are one of his favorite weapons to rob us of our peace of mind.

That is why Paul encourages us to take up "the shield of faith with which you will be able to extinguish all the flaming missiles of the evil one" (Eph. 6:16). In Paul's day the Roman shield, a piece of wood $2\frac{1}{2}$ feet by $4\frac{1}{2}$ feet, was covered with metal or water-soaked leather. The enemy would shoot an arrow that had been dipped in pitch and ignited. The only protection available against serious burns was this water-soaked shield. When the flaming missile struck the shield, it was immediately extinguished.

Paul is saying that when those anxiety attacks come, the most effective weapon a Christian has is faith: trusting in God's sovereign care over our lives.

Timothy, a young pastor, also had a problem with worry. Paul reminded him that "God hath not given us the spirit of fear; but of power, and of love, and of a sound mind" (2 Tim. 1:7, KJV). Sometimes we worry about *unfinished tasks*, those things we should be, but aren't, doing. It may be something as small as a dental checkup or reconciling our bank statement. Or our anxiety may be the result of projects that seem so large that we don't know where to begin. In either case the answer for our anxiety is action. Scheduling the appointment, balancing the checkbook, or (as we saw in chapter 3) breaking that project into manageable parts will remove unnecessary fear from our lives.

I am convinced that learning to handle worry in our lives will free us to experience guilt-free relaxation.[12]

2. Learn to delegate work.
It is impossible to enjoy periods of relaxation as long as you are trying to do both your job and everyone else's as well. Peter Drucker, the father of modern management, writes, "By now

managers everywhere have learned that decentralization strengthens top management. It makes it more effective and more capable of doing its own tasks."[13] Notice the words "its *own* tasks." An effective worker is one who has clearly defined his own responsibilities and focuses on them—not on everyone else's.

One common characteristic I see in workaholics is an inability to turn a task over to someone else *and leave it with them.* Sure, we may be able to perform our subordinate's job more effectively, but do we really want to? Most of us have enough to do without doing other people's work as well.

This concept of delegation is not limited to the workplace. Effective delegation of responsibilities in families, civic organizations, and churches is vital. The mother, the club president, or the church staff member who tries to do it all can never hope to experience guilt-free relaxation.

3. Set limits to your work.

Whether you are a housewife or a business executive, at times you must learn to say "enough" to your responsibilities. As we saw earlier, God has said that one day a week we are to say no to work or even the thought of work. I want to suggest that we should enjoy a "mini-Sabbath" every day. There should be a time each day when we quit working and enjoy the other aspects of our lives. Such breaks remind us there is more to life than work.

You may be a housewife who is consumed with the endless responsibilities of running a home. There are always meals to prepare, clothes to wash and fold, children to supervise. You could work twenty-four hours a day if you chose. But there needs to be a time in the day when you say "enough." It may be a period of time in the afternoon; it might be at nine o'clock in the evening. But you must set a limit to your work.

Those of you in the workplace may find it difficult to set limits to your work. You might be tempted to bring a briefcase full of work home with you at night "just in case you have some time." Or even if you leave the briefcase at work, you still have all kinds of "to do" files stored in your mind. It is difficult to read, watch television, or play with your children without thinking about those projects that need to be completed.

My friend Howard Hendricks says that he had a problem of mentally bringing home with him his work from the seminary. He was being robbed of guilt-free relaxation. So he designated a spot on his drive home where he threw out his mental briefcase full of concerns about his work. On the way back to work the next morning, his briefcase was always there, ready to jump in the car with him.

Author Jerry Jenkins once said that he refuses to bring *any* briefcase home with him—real or imaginary. His work remains at the office. Personally, I have found that that restriction is the only way I can hope to enjoy guilt-free relaxation.

4. Do something you want to do each day.
We all need something to anticipate. Just knowing that we will be able to spend thirty minutes or an hour doing something we want to do—reading a book, watching a television program, engaging in a sport—can compensate for the mundane or unpleasant tasks we must perform.

Management expert Harvey Mackay asks, "How do you overcome the inevitable drag on your spirits of doing tasks you hate but that have to be done? . . . If I have to do something I don't like, I make it a point to be especially nice to myself later by doing something I really do like. The same day."[14]

In my book *Choose Your Attitudes, Change Your Life*, I illustrated that principle from my own life. I related how Sundays were endurance contests for me—preaching two messages, attending committee meetings, and listening to the complaints of parishioners. But one way I get through the day is by looking forward to my Sunday night ritual: a bowl of popcorn, a diet Coke, and an old movie. It doesn't sound very spiritual. But it works. Just knowing I am going to do something I like helps me endure a grueling day.

I cannot begin to tell you the number of people who kidded me about that illustration after the book was released. Here was the typical response: "Oh, so you don't look forward to preaching? You enjoy eating and entertainment more than pastoring?"

Of course not. My point is that we all need some downtime each day to enjoy the other aspects of life apart from our work. Solomon certainly believed in that principle. In Ecclesiastes 2:24 he advised, "There is nothing better for a man than to eat and drink and tell himself that his labor is good. This also I have seen, that it is from the hand of God."

Solomon says we should view that bowl of popcorn, that soft drink, that good book, that movie, that football game—and the time to enjoy it—as a gracious gift from the hand of God.

5. Make time alone with God a part of each day.

Lest you think the above paragraph sounds too much like the hedonistic philosophy of "Eat, drink, and be merry, for tomorrow we die," let me continue Solomon's words in the next verse: "For who can eat and who can have enjoyment without Him?" (2:25). Solomon says that it is impossible to experience enjoyment (relaxation) apart from God.

Isn't it odd that many of us have turned our time with God through Bible study and prayer into a guilt-inducing ritual rather than a respite from the pressures of life? But God never intended us to view our time with him as a legalistic requirement, but as an escape from the pressures of life. We will discuss this further in the last section of the book.

I don't know where you are as you read this chapter. You may be on your way to work. You may be on your lunch break or on your way to an important appointment. But let me encourage you to close the book and for the next ten minutes refuse to worry about anything; reject any thoughts about your work or other obligations, and *relax*.

Think about the most enjoyable experience you have had in the past month or year. What is keeping you from repeating that experience again? Try to find a time on your calendar (after the ten minutes are up) to repeat that activity.

Visualize the event you are most looking forward to this week. If there is nothing, plan something!

Finally, thank God for the gift of life itself. Express gratitude for your family, your job, your health, and your material possessions with which to enjoy life.

Time's up. Now, didn't that feel good? Why not try it again tomorrow?

Maybe you're thinking, *I could afford to work less and relax more if I had more money.* If so, the next chapter is for you.

. . . . .

CHAPTER 6

Guilt-Free Money Management

S URVEY the best-seller list of Christian books, and you will notice an interesting phenomenon. The hottest titles are no longer those books dealing with the family, apologetics, addictions, eschatology, or the work of the Holy Spirit. The books zooming off the charts are about money and finances. Some are apocalyptic, prophesying a great economic collapse that will engulf both Christians and non-Christians alike. Others warn about the dangers of debt and explain how to live a debt-free existence. Still others talk about investing for the future—assuming there is any money left over at the end of the month to invest. A few even address the not-so-popular topic of giving.

Why are these books so much in demand? Part of their popularity is due to our national obsession with economics—an obsession fueled, in part, by our political process. Presidential elections are no longer decided on the basis of lofty ideology but on the most recent economic indicators: unemployment claims, inflation figures, and gross national product.

Consider the 1992 election. Although the nation had enjoyed twelve years of unprecedented economic growth, George Bush's 90 percent approval rating diminished to 30 percent, and he lost the election. Why? Not because of international instability or some drastic change in domestic policy, but because of a perceived sluggishness in the economy. Relentless warnings by the media that our nation was sliding into economic collapse caused Americans to believe it was time for a change. And those warnings worked.

The unfortunate by-product of those repeated warnings is that many Americans actually believe the doom-and-gloom predictions of whatever party is currently out of power. Thus, you see a continuing interest in these doomsday books that captivates both the secular and Christian markets.

But a more potent reason for our interest in financial matters is the anxiety many of us feel about our own finances. Many people's personal finances are in shambles. Consider these facts:

- Personal bankruptcies are at an all-time high, having climbed steadily since the 1950s.
- The number of American children living below the poverty line has increased from 14.9 percent in 1970 to 19 percent in 1990.
- Financial planner and psychologist Victoria Felton-Collins estimates that 90 percent of all divorces are caused by money.
- The life savings of the average fifty-year-old is $2,300.
- Our savings rate is only 4.5 percent (compared to 8.6 percent in 1973), while the Japanese save more than 15 percent.
- According to the Social Security Board 85 out of 100 reaching age 65 do not possess as much as $250.[1]

No wonder people are willing to purchase books that promise financial freedom in thirty days. The problem with most of the books is similar to the problem with many time-management books. Instead of relieving guilt—they induce more guilt! We are advised to accumulate staggering sums of money for our children's education and for retirement (even though these same advisers tell us the whole economic system is going to collapse, and all of our savings will be wiped out). We are told that we should never go into debt for anything. And at the same time, we are supposed to give a large portion of our income away to support God's work. The result is that many people throw up their hands in despair and give up hope of ever getting their financial house in order.

The Bible has a great deal to say about money. But unlike many Christian financial books, the Bible suggests some very reasonable guidelines about saving, debt, and giving that are designed to free Christians from financial concerns rather than enslave them.

THE BIBLE AND MONEY

Many Christians have a false idea that any concern about money is unspiritual. A "heavenly minded" person should not concern himself with "unrighteous mammon." Such a belief is in itself a source of unnecessary guilt. The Bible contains a wealth (pardon the pun) of information about money. Sixteen of Jesus' thirty-eight parables talk about money. One-sixth of Matthew, Mark, and Luke deal with money. You cannot turn a page of Proverbs without encountering the subject of finances. Why is there so much material in the Bible about money? Let me suggest three reasons:

First, managing our money well is a measure of our faithfulness to God. God has not called every person to be wealthy, but he has called us to be good stewards of what he has given us. Jesus said:

> He who is faithful in a very little thing is faithful also in much; and he who is unrighteous in a very little thing is unrighteous also in much. If therefore you have not been faithful in the use of unrighteous mammon, who will entrust the true riches to you? (Luke 16:10-11)

To Jesus, money was a very little thing compared to the true spiritual riches that await us in heaven. Nevertheless, our ability to handle such a "little thing" is a measure of our ability to handle the true riches that will one day be given to us.

Second, managing our money well is a powerful witness to unbelievers. A professing Christian who cannot pay his bills and is apprehensive about the future nullifies, in the eyes of the world, God's promise to provide for his children. To put it bluntly, who wants to serve a God who can't take care of his own children? Now the truth is God *has* promised to meet our needs—not our wants, but our needs. Paul confidently asserted, "My God shall supply all your needs according to His riches in glory in Christ Jesus" (Phil. 4:19). Unfortunately, many Christians are squandering God's provisions for their needs. And the result is a poor witness to the world.

A prominent businessman I know was noted for two things: his extravagant lifestyle and his failure to pay his debts. He continually owed a number of people in the church and the community money; yet he and his family took lavish vacations, wore the latest designer clothing, and drove new vehicles each year. I remember visiting a prospect for the church one time. When he discovered which church I represented, he said, "Oh, that is where ——— is a member. He's owed me two hundred dollars for the last three years, and he won't pay. If that's what it means to be a Christian, I'm not interested." How we manage our finances impacts our witness for Christ.

Finally, managing our money well frees us to serve Christ. Wise management of our finances is not an end unto itself but a means to an end. God does not necessarily want you rich or poor but *free* from concerns about money. The writer of Proverbs understood that when he wrote, "Two things I asked of Thee, do not refuse me before I die: Keep deception and lies far from me, give me neither poverty nor riches; feed me with the food that is my portion, lest I be full and deny Thee and say, "Who is the Lord?" or lest I be in want and steal, and profane the name of my God" (Prov. 30:7-9).

All this person wanted was not to have to worry about money. He realized that great wealth, as well as great poverty, could hinder him from concentrating on his relationship with God. Frankly, I think that the financial goal for every Christian should be this: not too much, not too little—just enough to allow us to pursue our real passion: serving Christ.

In their book *Your Money or Your Life*, authors Joe Dominguez and Vicki Robin tell of their decision to quit successful careers and live on six thousand dollars each of annual investment income. Their motivation for doing so was to free themselves from the rat race so that they could pursue their real passion of volunteer work and community service projects. Although the book was not written from a Christian perspective, it has a compelling message. Far too many people are working at jobs they really don't enjoy, to buy things they really don't need, to impress people they really don't like. We need to have a life purpose that extends beyond consumption. And when our life purpose enlarges beyond ourselves, we will find ourselves freed from many concerns about money.

I was recently thumbing through a most interesting book entitled *Enough*. In his review of the book, W. Randall Jones explains the philosophy of *Enough*, which may be what the writer of Proverbs 30 had in mind:

> The number one cause of stress is financial concern. The question is why? Of course the outcome of Mr. Clinton's economic plan causes worries. So do educating kids and job security, not to mention reaching those middle years when our mortality becomes all too real. But I think there is another big question, one we tend to think about less often. Could it be that most of us simply don't know when we have enough? One thing is certain, China's Tao Te Ching says, "He who knows he has enough is rich." Once you have defined enough, you won't have as much anxiety about getting more. This lessens that monster of financial anxiety and gives you control over your own financial goals.[2]

God wants us to enjoy a guilt-free existence in every life area, including our money management. Such an existence is only possible when we understand God's requirements for our finances and reject the unrealistic expectations of others— including many Christian financial "experts."

Three major areas of finances are prone to induce guilt in our lives: saving, debt, and giving. Let's see what the Bible says about each of these areas.

SAVING

Christians seem to go to one of two extremes in their view of saving and investing. They either underemphasize or over-emphasize the importance of setting aside money for future needs.

One view is that saving for the future is really unspiritual. After all, some argue, God will take care of our needs. Any kind of stockpile of money is only a hindrance to our trusting in God. Those with this view can find a lot of ammunition in Scripture. For example, consider Jesus' words:

> Do not lay up for yourselves treasures upon earth, where moth and rust destroy, and where thieves break in and steal. But lay up for yourselves treasures in heaven, where neither moth nor rust destroys, and where thieves do not break in or steal. . . . For this reason I say to you, do not be anxious for your life, as to what you shall eat, or what you shall drink; nor for your body, as to what you shall put on. Is not life more than food, and the body than clothing? Look at the birds of the air, that they do not sow, neither do they reap, nor gather into barns, and yet your heavenly Father feeds them. Are you not worth much more than they? . . . Therefore do not be anxious for tomorrow; for tomorrow will care for itself. Each day has enough trouble of its own. (Matt. 6:19-20, 25-26, 34)

Those are some pretty convincing words about being concerned about the future, aren't they? But before you run out and cash in your CDs or empty your retirement account, you might want to consider these words from the book of Proverbs:

> The rich man's wealth is his strong city: the destruction of the poor is their poverty. (Prov. 10:15, KJV)

> Four things are small on the earth, but they are exceedingly wise: The ants are not a strong folk, but they prepare their food in the summer. (Prov. 30:24-25)

> Go to the ant, O sluggard, observe her ways and be wise, which, having no chief, officer or ruler, prepares her food

in the summer, and gathers her provision in the harvest. How long will you lie down, O sluggard? When will you arise from your sleep? (Prov. 6:6-9)

Why is Solomon so hung up on ants? Because even a creature as small as an ant, with a brain so small it could not be seen with the naked eye, understands the importance of saving for the future!

However, saving for the future can be either good or evil—depending on our motivation. Let me point out three *wrong* reasons for saving money.

1. Greed

Simply defined, greed is the obsession for more. It is the opposite of contentment. Greed is built on the false assumption that "a little bit more" is all I need to satisfy me. In the area of saving, greed refers to the hoarding of money just for the sake of accumulating it, without any specific purpose in mind. However, saving is setting aside money for some specific future use.

Have you ever known people who are just in love with money itself? Solomon warned about the dangers of hoarding money:

> There is a grievous evil which I have seen under the sun: riches being hoarded by their owner to his hurt. When those riches were lost through a bad investment and he had fathered a son, then there was nothing to support him. As he had come naked from his mother's womb, so will he return as he came. He will take nothing from the fruit of his labor that he can carry in his hand. (Eccles. 5:13-15)

Solomon said it is folly to build your life around hoarding money, because it can be so easily lost. Recently I read an article in *Money* magazine about a retired gentleman who had spent his life working endlessly to amass a retirement nest egg of $350,000. About seven years ago the man was contacted by a salesman from a savings and loan institution who "just happened to notice" that the retiree's money was sitting in some low-yielding certificates of deposit. The salesman persuaded the man to shift his money into a higher-yielding annuity. Unfortunately, the insurance company that sponsored the annuity went bankrupt, and now the man has his account frozen. Although he has been told that he will eventually get his money, he replies, "Tell the reformers to hurry up. I'll be eighty in September. I can't wait forever."[3]

Money can be easily lost. Years earlier, Solomon wrote, "Do not wear yourself out to get rich; have the wisdom to show restraint. Cast but a glance at riches, and they are gone, for they will surely sprout wings and fly off to the sky like an eagle" (Prov. 23:4-5, NIV).

2. Poor planning

It may strike some people as a contradiction to say that saving can be the result of poor planning. But consider the couple who find themselves two years away from having their first child in college or three years away from retirement. Because of a failure to plan ahead, they suddenly have to accumulate in a few years what they should have spent many years in planning. The result is either an unrealistic goal like trying to save 50 percent of their income or the temptation to participate in high-risk investments that are almost guaranteed to fail. Proverbs 20:4 says, "The sluggard does not plow after the autumn, so he begs during the harvest and has nothing." In other words, a fool does not make adequate preparation for the future.

3. Protection

Some people have protection from adversity as their motivation for saving. They think that if they can just accumulate enough money, they can then relax and not fear any future problems.

Certainly, adequate reserves of cash can be a protection from the uncertainties of life. Financial experts recommend that we keep three to six months' living expenses in reserve for emergencies. But wise planning is not the same as trusting in money alone to protect us from life's adversities. No amount of money is sufficient to protect us from all potential problems.

For example, what about those who are suddenly disabled and have no disability insurance? Could they reasonably expect to save enough money to protect them from a lifetime of unemployment?

What of those who have lost medical insurance, and then a year later, a child is diagnosed with an illness requiring hundreds of thousands of dollars of medical care? How quickly would their savings be eroded?

Or what if someone is accidentally killed in an automobile accident and the driver is sued for several million dollars? Could anyone's investments cover that?

Money can protect us from some problems, but not all. That is why Solomon wrote, "The wealth of the rich is their fortified city; they *imagine* it an unscalable wall" (Prov. 18:11, NIV, emphasis mine).

To trust in money rather than in God for our protection is foolishness. That was the error of the rich fool in Luke 12. After spending his life accumulating money, he said to himself:

> "Soul, you have many goods laid up for many years to come; take your ease, eat, drink and be merry." But God said to him, "You fool! This very night your soul is required of you; and now who will own what you have prepared?" (12:19-20)

To trust in riches rather than in God is the essence of idolatry. The psalmist reminds us that only God can protect us from the disasters of life: "Offer to God a sacrifice of thanksgiving, and pay your vows to the Most High; and call upon *Me* in the day of trouble; *I* shall rescue you, and you will honor Me" (Psalm 50:14-15; emphasis mine).

Are there any legitimate reasons for a Christian to save and invest for the future? I believe the Bible gives at least two motivations for saving:

1. To meet the future needs of one's family
While we should not put our faith in money to protect us, our wise use of what God has already provided is one way he will meet our future needs. And that means consuming less than we make. Solomon wrote, "There is precious treasure and oil in the dwelling of the wise, but a foolish man swallows it up" (Prov. 21:20). In other words, only a fool spends everything he has and makes no provision for future need. We have a responsibility to provide for the needs of our family—both present and future. Those needs include the basics—food, clothing, housing, medical care—as well as educational expenses, recreational pursuits, and dozens of other items. The apostle Paul warned, "But if anyone does not provide for his own, and especially for those of his household, he has denied the faith, and is worse than an unbeliever" (1 Tim. 5:8).

2. To provide for special needs in the church
We will talk more about giving in the final section of this chapter. But the Bible says that one reason we should save is so that we can meet special needs that might arise in God's work. The Bible teaches weekly giving to the church. But the Bible also teaches weekly saving of some of our funds that are to be earmarked for unexpected needs in the church. In 1 Corinthians 16:2 Paul said, "On the first day of every week let each one

of you put aside and save, as he may prosper, that no collections be made when I come." Notice the word *save*. Paul was encouraging the Corinthians to save some money for a specific need above the regular needs of the church at Corinth—a gift for the saints in Jerusalem.

When I entered junior high school, I embarked on an ambitious savings plan. By the time I was a sophomore in high school, I had accumulated an impressive amount of money through a part-time job and from playing my accordion at different functions. (Yes, back then people actually *paid* to hear the accordion. One of my deacons recently gave me a good definition of an optimist: "An accordionist with a beeper.")

I was also involved with a small church that had a vision for a large bus ministry to reach the poorer segments of the community. They had a worthy vision but no money. One Sunday morning the pastor made an appeal for people to give sacrificially, and I happily gave all that I had saved to that worthy project. The money was eventually raised and a successful ministry begun. Why? It would not have happened unless a number of Christians had consumed less than they had earned over a period of time and contributed that surplus to this ministry.

From time to time there will be special needs in any church. Funds may be needed for a building program, a mission offering, more pews for the sanctuary, or a new van. Where should that money come from? I believe that instead of borrowing the money, it should come from the surplus that Christians have accumulated for this purpose.

A REASONABLE GOAL

How much should I be saving to meet the future needs of my family as well as future ministry needs that might arise? Many financial experts tell us that we should be saving 10 to 15 percent of our income for retirement purposes alone. And that doesn't take into consideration other future family needs like college costs, medical catastrophes, or other needs that might arise. There is no standard answer that fits everyone's situation. Proverbs 15:22 encourages us to seek godly counsel in every area of life, including our finances: "Without consultation, plans are frustrated, but with many counselors they succeed."

The most important things to remember about saving are (a) it is a scriptural principle to save for the future and (b) saving is never to replace trusting in God to meet our needs.

DEBT-FREE LIVING?

In this book we are attempting to explain what the biblical requirements are in different life areas and also expose some of the myths about these areas that cause illegitimate guilt. A number of financial experts in the Christian community are teaching that debt is wrong for a Christian in any circumstances. They say it is wrong to borrow money for a car, an education, a house, a church building, or anything else. One well-known Christian financial expert writes, "God's Word tells us that his plan for us is to be debt-free. . . . I hope to show that is still God's plan and that it is entirely possible, even in this present generation."[4]

Some other experts moderate this view by saying that Christians should only borrow for those items that are appreciating in value (like real estate—at least until recently).

The problem I have with this blanket statement is twofold. First, I have a difficult time finding an absolute prohibition against borrowing money in the Bible. And second, such blanket prohibitions do not recognize the differing economic circumstances of individuals. The result is that many Christians are feeling unnecessarily guilty about their financial situation.

First, let's look at what the Bible does say about debt. In the Bible debt is sometimes called surety, and it can be defined as "a pledge or object in the possession of the debtor handed over to the creditor as a guarantee for his debt."[5] For example, if I borrow the money to purchase a new car for twenty thousand dollars, I need to ask myself if I would be able to repay that loan under any circumstance. If I lost my job, would I still be able to pay for the car? If I have other assets that could cover that indebtedness, then I am really not in debt in the biblical sense of the word. To be in debt is to make a pledge without any certain way to repay that debt. And the Bible warns us about the danger of making that kind of pledge:

> My son, if you have become surety for your neighbor, have given a pledge for a stranger . . . do this then, my son, and deliver yourself; since you have come into the hand of your neighbor, go, humble yourself, and importune your neighbor. (Prov. 6:1, 3)

> A man lacking in sense pledges, and becomes surety in the presence of his neighbor. (Prov. 17:18)

> The rich rules over the poor, and the borrower becomes the lender's slave. (Prov. 22:7)

> Do not be among those who give pledges, among those who become sureties for debts. If you have nothing with which to pay, why should he take your bed from under you? (Prov. 22:26-27)

> Do not boast about tomorrow, for you do not know what a day may bring forth. (Prov. 27:1)

The Bible is full of warning about indebtedness. And with good reason. Our national debt is increasing $10,000 every second. Consumer debt alone exceeds $735 billion in 1990—42 percent more than in 1985 and 146 percent more than in 1980. Our mortgages, car loans, and credit card debts, coupled with our low savings rate, make many of us an economic disaster waiting to happen. Recent surveys have shown that most Americans could not survive more than four weeks without a job.[6] We are shackled by debt.

And yet some debt has almost become imperative in order for us to live. Very few people could hope to accumulate enough money to buy a home—or even an automobile—with cash. Many parents find that they need to borrow some money, if not the entire amount, to finance their children's education. Churches rarely are able to raise in advance all of the money needed for a major capital project. If they wait until they have all the cash in hand, they may find that escalating costs have negated any interest savings.

When then is debt wrong? I believe the Bible teaches debt is wrong when

1. *Our debt presumes* heavily *on the future*

Notice the operative word here is *heavily*. All plans presume somewhat on the future. Before we plan what we will do tomorrow, we assume we will be alive and that the Lord will not return (though our plans should always allow for either contingency). But if we go into debt saying, "I can repay this debt *if* I get a 15 percent raise, the economy improves dramatically, and Aunt Bessie dies by January first," *that* is presuming on the future! Again, Proverbs says, "Do not boast about tomorrow, for you do not know what a day may bring forth" (Prov. 27:1).

2. Our debt places our welfare or our family's welfare at risk
Ask yourself, If I am not able to repay this debt, what is the worst thing that could happen? For example, could this unpaid debt cause you to lose your home? If so, you are putting your family in jeopardy. That's why Solomon asked the question "If you have nothing with which to pay, why should he take your bed from under you?" (Prov. 22:27).

3. Our debt causes us to default on our promise to pay
Many people point to Romans 13:8 as an absolute prohibition against debt: "Owe nothing to anyone except to love one another." Yet when you examine the context of that passage, you find that Paul is addressing the subject of paying taxes. He is simply saying, "Don't be delinquent in paying what you owe the government." Paul then extends that principle beyond the government: Don't be delinquent in paying what you owe anyone.

If you borrow money from a bank to purchase a home, you will sign a promissory note with that lending institution. The terms of the contract are that you will pay X number of dollars each month for a prescribed length of time. As long as you meet the terms of that note, you are not being delinquent in your finances. You are simply fulfilling a promise. It is when we default on a note that we "owe" another person as Paul describes in Romans 13:8.

4. Our debt causes us stress and anxiety
Remember, our goal in guilt-free money management is not wealth or poverty but *freedom* to serve Christ. Any financial transaction that causes unnecessary stress or anxiety is wrong. In 2 Timothy 2:4 Paul says, "No soldier in active service entan-

gles himself in the affairs of everyday life, so that he may please the one who enlisted him as a soldier."

A good friend of mine in my former church hit it big during the oil boom of the 1980s. During that insane time in our national life, he (like many others) leveraged his business with a large debt to enlarge his company. He also purchased something he had always wanted—his own King Air, a two-engine airplane, complete with hangar and a private pilot. He loved taking off every weekend with his wife to exotic locations around the world. Life was never so good!

Then the bust came. With these massive debts hanging over him and consuming every bit of spare cash he had, he found himself emotionally strangled by his indebtedness. It distracted him from his family, his friendships, and his church involvement. Finally, he came to the conclusion that he needed to sell his airplane and some other assets to eliminate the debt and free him to serve God and his family.

I believe God wants us to eliminate anything in our lives—including debt—that is preventing us from serving Christ completely. The writer of Hebrews admonishes us to "lay aside every encumbrance, and the sin which so easily entangles us, and let us run with endurance the race that is set before us" (Heb. 12:1).

GIVING

No discussion of money management from a biblical perspective would be complete without addressing the subject of giving. Whenever I preach about this topic, I can sense people beginning to tense up. I tell my congregation that stewardship messages are a lot like root canals—they may be necessary, but they surely are painful!

One reason they are painful is because many Christians feel

extremely guilty about their lack of financial support to the church. And some of that guilt is well deserved. Recent studies have shown that those in my denomination, the Southern Baptist Convention, give 1.67 percent of their income to the church. I have an article in my file claiming that if every church member in America lost his job and tithed from the welfare payments, contributions to the church would rise by 35 percent. Some guilt about stewardship is legitimate!

But some of the guilt about giving stems from a legalistic perspective that turns giving into a ritual rather than an expression of worship. Some time ago, a Christian who has been most generous to our church approached me about a "problem" he was having. Through the counsel of another Christian leader, this man had been giving a tenth of his gross receipts (rather than the profit) from his business to the church. Now he was facing increased taxes, and he was afraid that for a while he would only be able to tithe his net income rather than his gross income. He was eaten up with guilt, afraid that he was disobeying God and might suffer his discipline. I resisted the self-serving urge I felt to admonish him to continue his practice or face the wrath of God and instead helped him to see God's perspective about giving.

Let me share with you the same five principles I explained to him about stewardship that might release you from guilt you feel about giving.

1. Giving is an act of worship.

God wants us to give as an act of worship, not to satisfy some legalistic requirement. In 2 Corinthians 9:7 Paul summarizes the way we are to give: "Let each one do just as he has purposed in his heart; not grudgingly or under compulsion; for God loves a *cheerful* giver." The word *cheerful* comes from the Greek word that means "hilarious." God wants us to enjoy hilarious giving—giving that flows out of a grateful heart for all God has done for us.

In Mark 12:41-44 we find a word about Jesus' attitude about giving:

> And He sat down opposite the treasury, and began observing how the multitude were putting money into the treasury; and many rich people were putting in large sums. And a poor widow came and put in two small copper coins, which amount to a cent. And calling His disciples to Him, He said to them, "Truly I say to you, this poor widow put in more than all the contributors to the treasury; for they all put in out of their surplus, but she, out of her poverty, put in all she owned, all she had to live on.

Notice that Jesus commended this widow's gift, even though it was made to the treasury, which represented the corrupt religious system of Jesus' day—a religious system that ultimately put Christ to death. Yet the widow saw her gift as to the Lord, not to man. Yes, those religious leaders were misusing those funds, and someday they would have to answer to God for that. But that was not her concern. Her responsibility was to be faithful in giving. She saw her offering as a gift to God.

Occasionally, someone will argue with me about tithing—giving 10 percent of one's income to God's work. They say, "We are not under the law; therefore, we do not have to tithe." That is true—we are not under the law. We live under grace. And if we have truly experienced the grace of Jesus Christ, we should ask ourselves, How much can I give? not How little can I get by with? If you are sincerely trying to please the Lord, a natural question is going to be How much does God want me to give? An honest look at the Bible reveals that the tithe is a standard for giving.

The tithe was a standard of giving for Abraham—who lived five hundred years before the Mosaic law. Abraham gave a tenth of his spoils in victory to God's priest, Melchizedek (Gen. 14). Abraham's grandson Jacob declared in Genesis 28:22, "Of all that Thou dost give me I will surely give a tenth to Thee." The Mosaic law prescribed that the tithe was also a standard of giving as found in Leviticus 27:30. Finally, Jesus Christ commended the tithe in Matthew 23:23. The tithe, therefore, can be seen as a standard that transcends any one particular era in biblical history.

In 1 Corinthians 16:2, Paul commands every Christian to give as God has prospered him. For most of us that will be at least a tenth of our income. Paul is saying that our giving is an act of worship—expressing gratitude to God for the way he has prospered us.

2. *Giving reminds us that all of our possessions belong to God.*

Although the tithe is the starting place of our giving, we should remember that God is not only interested in 10 percent of our money but in all of it. Second Corinthians 5:10 reminds us that as Christians we will one day stand before the judgment seat of Christ and give an account of our time, our abilities, our money, and all that God has entrusted to us. Giving reminds us that all we have really belongs to God and is simply on loan to us.

3. *Giving allows us to prepare for eternity.*

Perhaps you have heard the old saying You can't take it with you. That's true. But you can send it on ahead of you!

Remember the parable in Luke 16 about the dishonest steward who knew he was about to be fired and prepared for his future unemployment in a unique way? He quickly discounted all of his employer's accounts receivable in order to make friends with his employer's customers, hoping they would give him a job when he was laid off. Although Jesus did not commend this steward's dishonesty, he did compliment the steward for having the wisdom to use present opportunities to secure his future. And so Jesus advised all of us to "make friends for yourselves by means of the mammon of unrighteousness; that when it fails, they may receive you into the eternal dwellings" (Luke 16:9).

What was Jesus saying? When we give to support God's work, we are ensuring that there will be people who welcome us into heaven by saying, "You don't know me, but because of your gift, I heard the gospel and believed. Thank you for making all of this possible." What a motivation to give!

4. Giving increases our interest in God's kingdom.

Earlier we looked at Matthew 6:19-20 in which Jesus warned against stockpiling money on earth at the expense of investing it in God's kingdom. He closed by saying, "For where your treasure is, there will your heart be also" (6:21).

Had I been Jesus, I would not have said it that way. I would have reversed it: "For where your *heart* is, there will your *treasure* be also." That makes more sense. Our money is where our heart is. Or, to put it another way, we spend our money on the things we really love.

When I was in high school, I started dating my future wife seriously. Within a few months, I was faced with a big decision: what to purchase for her upcoming birthday. I polled my friends and family, and they all agreed. Perfume was the most romantic gift a guy could buy for a girl.

So the next Saturday I went downtown to Neiman-Marcus and found a bottle of Estée Lauder perfume. The saleslady promised that Amy would faint over such an extravagant gift. But I was the one who nearly fainted when I saw the price. I calculated that the bottle of perfume would cost me an entire week's paycheck from my part-time job at a local Christian bookstore. But one week of mopping the floor and cleaning the bathroom was a small price to pay for my truelove. I was delighted to spend my money on Amy. In fact, during my dating days I could not hold on to any money. I was happily spending every penny on her. Why? Because I loved her. My money was where my heart was.

Perhaps Jesus thought that was too obvious. Instead, he reminded us of a converse truth: Wherever our money is, is where our heart will be. To the Hebrew, the word *heart* did not refer to the emotional center of man's being, but to his mind. A paraphrase of this verse might read, "For where your money is, there will your mind be also."

If your money is in the stock market, guess where your mind will be. If the bulk of your money is in your home, guess where your thoughts will naturally gravitate. If the majority of your disposable income each week is spent on recreational pursuits, guess what will consume your daydreams. Our thoughts follow our money.

In Colossians 3:2 Paul writes, "Set your mind on the things above, not on the things that are on earth." For most people that is easier said than done! The everyday responsibilities of life—family, work, relaxation, financial concerns—war against our centering our thoughts and affections around God's kingdom. Jesus is saying that one way to become more "heavenly minded" is to start investing our money in God's work.

5. Giving brings God's blessings into our lives.
Many of us vehemently denounce the teaching of the televangelists who promise material prosperity in exchange for a gift to their ministry. Yet I am afraid we may have thrown out the proverbial baby with the bathwater. God *does* promise blessings to those who give. Malachi 3:10 encourages us to "bring the whole tithe into the storehouse, so that there may be food

in My house, and test Me now in this," says the Lord of hosts, "if I will not open for you the windows of heaven, and pour out for you a blessing until it overflows."

God's blessings may not always be material. Our blessing from giving may be the deep sense of satisfaction from knowing that our material resources are being used for eternal good.

But many times God's blessings *are* material. I recently had lunch with someone who shared his experience in giving with me. A few years ago, he and his wife were scraping the bottom financially. They were down to their final two hundred dollars in the bank when the pastor announced that the church was in financial difficulty. Grateful for the way the church had ministered to their family, the couple decided to give their last two hundred dollars to the church. And they did so happily, grateful for the opportunity to play a part in meeting the church's need. He went on to relate the many ways God had supernaturally blessed his family—including financially. Giving does allow us to experience God's blessings.

I am not saying that giving will always result in material wealth. If I could promise that, then giving would not be an act of worship but a shrewd business proposition.

But I am promising that if you are faithful in your giving, you will be relieved of much of the anxiety you may be feeling about money right now. Regular, proportionate giving reminds us that all of our resources are not ours but are on loan to us from God.

There seems to be a direct link between money and marriage. Statistics tell us that for every two marriages today one divorce occurs. And up to 80 percent of those divorces are said to be the result of money disputes. Many times these disputes stem from unrealistic expectations about intimacy and submission that partners bring into a marriage. And often these unrealistic expectations come from the Christian community, as we will see in the next chapter.

CHAPTER 7

. . . . .

Guilt-Free
Marriage

I have dreaded writing this chapter for weeks. Why? First, I
know that once these words are set in type they will return
to me like a giant boomerang, via my wife! But I also fear
that some ideas I express could be either intentionally or unin-
tentionally misunderstood and used to shatter the fragile alli-
ance that exists in so many marriages today.

I begin by expressing my firm conviction that marriage is a
gift from God. While there are some who have the gift of
remaining single, God's plan for most of us is that we have a
lifelong companion to complement us. What I am about to say
will appear heretical at first. But I want you to give it serious
attention before you reject it:

A relationship with God is not enough to satisfy all of your needs.

Surprised? You shouldn't be. Such a statement is very biblical. After God's climactic work of creating man, he said, "It is
not good for the man to be alone" (Gen. 2:18). What a strange
statement! Adam was hardly alone. He was enjoying a perfect

relationship with God—one that had not yet been ruined by sin. Yet God said that was not enough. Why?

Adam was created as a spiritual being. Thus, he would never find ultimate contentment without a spiritual relationship with his Creator. But, like all of us, Adam was *more* than a spiritual being. He also needed an intimate relationship with another person.[1] And God's plan for satisfying that need was through the marriage relationship:

> "I will make him a helper suitable for him. . . ." So the Lord God caused a deep sleep to fall upon the man, and he slept; then He took one of his ribs, and closed up the flesh at that place. And the Lord God fashioned into a woman the rib which He had taken from the man, and brought her to the man. (Gen. 2:18; 21-22)

I believe that one of God's provisions for us to experience completion or "closure" (as we have talked about throughout this book) is through the marriage relationship. Yet, for many people, marriage is a major source of guilt. Some of the guilt is legitimate. Much is illegitimate.

Those who write and speak extensively on the family warn that Christians' attitudes about marriage and family are being shaped by the world. Unfortunately, that is true. Television shows pour into our living rooms night after night, suggesting that lifelong commitments are a thing of the past. One actress is quoted as saying, "To me, breakup and divorce seem like the norm. Whenever I meet people whose parents are still together, I'm amazed. They're freaks. They make me nervous. Seeing people still married after twenty years is like watching a TV show."

But our ideas about marriage are not only shaped by the secular media; they are also influenced by our Christian culture.

Christian books, magazines, seminars, radio messages, and sermons are telling us what our marriages should look like. And the result is that many believers have inflated expectations about their own responsibilities, as well as their mate's, that result in guilt, disappointment, and disharmony.

Christian culture may be as much responsible for divorces among believers as the secular culture because of these inflated expectations. In this chapter we are going to attempt to diffuse some myths about marriage that result in unrealistic expectations and examine what God's Word teaches are our responsibilities in marriage.

SEVEN MYTHS THAT CREATE UNNECESSARY GUILT

Certain myths about marriage are among the sources of unnecessary guilt. All of these myths are deeply rooted in Christian culture.

Myth #1: "Marriage is not just two people marrying but two families marrying."

Cynthia and her family had been visiting our church for a while. They were members of another denomination but felt they were being ministered to by our church. Their former denomination was quite different in expressions of worship, so they carefully prayed about a change in churches before they made any decision. But one Sunday morning, the entire family presented themselves for membership, and they became actively involved in our fellowship.

Several weeks later, Cynthia called. She was very upset. Her mother had expressed grave disappointment over her daughter joining our church. Cynthia's mother had reminded her of her "Christian duty" to honor her parents. And forsaking the church of her childhood was anything but honoring! Cynthia was deeply disturbed. On the one hand she knew that she and her family had made the right decision in joining our church. But she also wanted to be obedient to God and honor her parents.

That afternoon I shared with Cynthia a simple but important principle from God's Word about marriage. It is a principle that can relieve you of unnecessary guilt whenever you are faced with a similar situation with your parents or siblings.

We must sever the emotional strings with our mother, father, and siblings in order to enjoy a happy, guilt-free marriage. By severing emotional ties, I don't mean that we forget them, abandon them, refrain from spending time with them, or refuse to care for them. We simply must realize that when we marry, we are creating a new home that deserves our *primary* allegiance.

We find this principle clearly explained in Genesis 2:24: "For this cause a man shall leave his father and his mother, and shall cleave to his wife; and they shall become one flesh." Notice the phrase *shall leave*. Moses did not instruct the man to invite his future bride to come and be a part of his existing family. Instead, the bond between parent and child had to be severed before a new bond could be formed between husband and wife.

Unfortunately, such severing is not always easy. Parents will resort to all kinds of manipulative techniques to retain control over their married children. Constantly reminding children of their sacrifices, bribing grandchildren, offering financial help, and pouting over perceived slights are just some of the tools parents use to retain emotional control over their children. As long as children are constantly worrying about what "mom and dad" think, they will never be free to develop the guilt-free intimacy that God desires for them.

This principle is especially important when so many couples are facing the decision about what to do with their aging parents. Just as our parents cared for us when we were dependents, we have now reversed roles and are caring for our parents as dependents. Certainly that is a valid application of Exodus 20:12: "Honor your father and your mother, that your days may be prolonged in the land which the Lord your God gives you." But such care might have to come in the form of nursing homes or shared responsibility with other siblings.

Myth #2: "When I marry, I give up my own identity and interests."

If you read enough Christian books about marriage, or listen to enough sermons, you will discover a common theme: Emotional oneness is essential for a successful marriage. What is emotional "oneness"? For many of these experts, "oneness" is "sameness." We will never enjoy intimacy with our spouse until we become exactly like our spouse, they imply.

One noted Christian author describes this scenario as a prescription for a disastrous marriage: "When Robert and Sherry were engaged, they spent hundreds of hours and thousands of dollars preparing for their marriage ceremony. But neither spent much time preparing for making their marriage work. When they married, they assumed they had the same plan for achieving oneness. But in reality they had no plan at all for building their home together. Bliss turned to burden as they struggled through everything from how to handle finances, to how to spend a Saturday afternoon."[2]

The inference here is that until Robert and Sherry agree on how to spend their money and Saturday afternoons, they will never be happy. Or possibly, since they don't agree, they should have never been married to begin with.

The truth is that God never intended for our spouse to be like us. Yes, there are certainly some basic beliefs and goals that a couple should share in common, like a commitment to serving Jesus Christ. The prophet Amos asked a logical question: "Can two walk together, except they be agreed?" (Amos 3:3, KJV). But beyond those bedrock beliefs, we should celebrate, rather than condemn, our differences.

Wives, God never intended your husband to be just like you. Husbands, God does not desire your wife to be a female version of you. One of you is enough! Look carefully at the biblical account of the creation of the first woman:

> And the man gave names to all the cattle, and to the birds of the sky, and to every beast of the field, but for Adam there was not found a helper suitable for him. . . . And the Lord God fashioned into a woman the rib which He had taken from the man, and brought her to the man." (Gen. 2:20, 22)

Notice the words *a helper suitable for him.* The phrase can be literally translated (as it is in the Revised Standard Version) "a help as *opposite* him." God intended for our mates to complement us, not to duplicate us.

I don't care how many Marriage Encounter weekends you and your mate attend; chances are you will never agree on how to spend your money or your Saturdays. *But that's OK!* Our differences can strengthen us rather than divide us.

In 1 Corinthians 12, Paul explains that Christians have different spiritual gifts. The result of these differing gifts is that the body of Christ can operate more effectively. Just as there are many parts of the physical body, there are many parts of the body of Christ—all essential to its effective operation. "But now God has placed the members, each one of them, in the body, just as He desired. And if they were all one member, where would the body be? But now there are many members, but one body" (1 Cor. 12:18-20).

What a perfect picture of a marriage! Genesis 2:24 reminds

us that in marriage we become "one flesh" or "one body." And yet, in that unity there remains diversity. When we try to make our spouse more like ourself, we are actually working against God's plan for our marriage.

Myth #3: "My spouse and I should enjoy sex in the same way."

Read Ann Landers or Dear Abby for any period of time, and you will discover that sexual differences are a major cause of marital disunity. Let me illustrate what I mean by "differences":

> My spouse is a sex maniac. He (she) wants sex five times a week.
>
> My spouse must have a medical problem or is having an affair. He (she) only wants sex twice a month.
>
> My spouse and I can never enjoy mutual orgasms.
>
> I wish my spouse were more creative in his (her) love-making.
>
> I wish my spouse were not so bizarre in his (her) love-making.

Few areas of marriage are as sensitive and as shrouded in secrecy as the sexual area of our relationships. A recent article in *U.S. News and World Report* on sexuality claims that "millions of Americans are unhappy with their intimate lives."[3] What is the source of such dissatisfaction?

In a word—comparison. We are doomed to discontent in our sexual lives as long as we compare our spouse to other lovers we may have experienced, as we compare our marriage to some "norm" we think exists, or as we compare our mate's needs to our own. Let me expand on these ideas further.

MISTAKE #1: COMPARING OUR SPOUSE TO OTHER SEXUAL PARTNERS. I was fascinated by two statements in the above-mentioned article on sexual desire. First, Americans are engaging in premarital sex in record numbers. Today, more than 80 percent of women and 90 percent of men now engage in premarital intercourse.[4] (As a pastor, my own observation is that those percentages are the same for Christians and non-Christians alike.) Second, record numbers of couples are dissatisfied with their sex lives. Is there a correlation between premarital sex and sexual dissatisfaction in relationships? I think there is.

I believe one reason God prohibits premarital sex is that he knows we cannot help but compare partners. In both premarital and extramarital sex, there is an extra excitement that is part of the "forbidden fruit" syndrome. When such excitement is not translated into the marriage relationship, discontent is sure to grow. A person who refrains from premarital or extramarital intercourse does not fall into the snare of such comparison.

MISTAKE #2: COMPARING OUR SEXUAL RELATIONSHIPS TO OTHERS'. We also make a mistake when we think there is some sexual "norm" that our marriage should be attaining. The fact is that most experts in the area of sexual dysfunction refuse to define what a "normal" sexual appetite is. Some couples may enjoy sex daily, others weekly, still others monthly. Certainly age, life circumstances, and individual physiological differences make defining what is "normal" impossible.

According to God's Word, the only "standard" of sexual desire we need to consider is what is pleasing to our mate. Paul wrote:

> Let the husband fulfill his duty to his wife, and likewise also the wife to her husband. The wife does not have authority over her own body, but the husband does; and likewise also the husband does not have authority over his own body, but the wife does. Stop depriving one another. (1 Cor. 7:3-5)

Paul is saying that as long as we are satisfied—and our mate is satisfied—it doesn't matter what Kinsey, Masters and Johnson, or Dr. Ruth say!

In his book *The Challenge of the Disciplined Life*, Richard Foster observes that one of the greatest dangers of movies, television, and blatant pornography is that they portray sex unrealistically. Sex is always seen as exhilarating. If the walls aren't shaking every time you and your spouse make love, something is wrong! "Sex in the real world is a mixture of tenderness and halitosis, love and fatigue, ecstasy and disappointment."[5]

MISTAKE #3: COMPARING OUR SEXUAL NEEDS TO OUR SPOUSE'S NEEDS. As we saw in the previous section, God created us different from our mates. And those differences manifest themselves in our sexual likes and dislikes. Dennis Rainey has catalogued some of those differences in a helpful chart. Obviously, they are not true in every case but generally seem to highlight the differences between men and women.[6]

If you and your spouse are able to enjoy simultaneous orgasms (just like in the movies)—*congratulations*. If you enjoy the same type and frequency of intercourse, you don't need to read this section (you should be writing this chapter). But if you are like most couples, you probably don't experience simultaneous orgasms. And you probably express your sexuality differently than your spouse. Celebrate your differences. Enjoy one another. Meet each other's needs. And most important, *quit comparing!* The apostle Paul calls comparison "stupidity" (2 Cor. 10:12, TLB).

Myth #4: "My spouse and I should have the same attitude about money."

Imagine that your Aunt Agnes suddenly dies and leaves you a windfall of ten thousand dollars. What would you do with the money—save it, buy a new car, take a vacation? What would your spouse want to do with the money? What do you want to

Differences in Sexuality

	MEN	WOMEN
Orientation	Physical Compartmentalized Physical oneness Variety Sex is high priority	Relational Wholistic Emotional oneness Security Other priorities may be higher
Stimulation	Sight Smell Body-centered	Touch Attitudes Actions Words Person-centered
Needs	Respect Admiration Physically needed Not to be put down	Understanding Love Emotionally needed Time
Sexual Response	Acyclical Quick excitement Initiates (usually) Difficult to distract	Cyclical Slow excitement Responds (usually) Easily distracted
Orgasm	Propagation of species Shorter, more intense Physically-oriented Orgasm usually needed for satisfaction	Propagation of oneness Longer, more in depth Emotionally-oriented Satisfaction possible without orgasm

bet that you and your mate would have different ideas on the subject?

As I mentioned earlier, numerous studies have suggested that 90 percent of divorces are precipitated by conflicts over money.

Most disagreements arise from different attitudes about money—attitudes deeply rooted in one's past. For some people, money is a tool to buy those things that make life easier and more satisfying. Someone who grew up in a household with that attitude, chances are, will feel that way about money.

For others, money is a commodity to be invested for future needs. Again, if that was the dominant view in one's parents' home, that attitude will be the same for the grown-up child. If you are like me and grew up in a home where one parent was a saver and the other a spender, you are probably as schizoid as I am about money!

Because your attitudes about money have been shaped by past experiences, marital counseling won't easily change your perspective. So quit feeling guilty that you and your mate view money differently! What *is* the best way to spend that ten thousand dollar windfall—spend it or invest it? Why not compromise with your mate? Spend six thousand dollars and save four thousand dollars. Such compromise will bring needed balance in your life.

As we saw in chapter 5, the Bible gives something of a balance between saving and spending. When Solomon was a young man, he wrote about the importance of saving money: "Go to the ant, O sluggard, observe her ways and be wise, which, having no chief, officer or ruler, prepares her food in the summer, and gathers her provision in the harvest" (Prov. 6:6-8). Yet, when Solomon was older, he expressed a more liberal attitude about money:

> Here is what I have seen to be good and fitting: to eat, to drink and enjoy oneself in all one's labor in which he toils under the sun during the few years of his life which God has given him; for this is his reward. Furthermore, as for every man to whom God has given riches and wealth, He

has also empowered him to eat from them and to receive his reward and rejoice in his labor; this is the gift of God. (Eccles. 5:18-19)

To paraphrase—you'd better have a blast while you last!

The wisest man that ever lived says we should save money. Yet he also says it is futile to hoard money and not enjoy the few years that God has given us. Contradictory? Not necessarily. God wants balance in our lives. And one way he helps us achieve that balance is by giving us a spouse who doesn't see things just the way we do.

Myth #5: "If we truly love each other, we will never be attracted to other people."

In the next section, we will be examining God's requirements for marriage—and at the top of the list is sexual fidelity. But such fidelity does not mean we cannot appreciate someone else's beauty, sense of humor, intellect, or spiritual commitment. After all, they are the work of God's creation. In 1 Timothy 4:4 Paul affirmed that "everything created by God is good, and nothing is to be rejected, if it is received with gratitude."

Admittedly, there is a fine line to be drawn between appreciation and lust. Whenever our thoughts about another person degenerate into fantasy, a mental undressing, and imaginary intercourse, we have crossed the line.

Additionally, whenever we unfavorably compare our spouse to someone else—either mentally or verbally, we are sowing the seeds of discontent in our marriage.

Myth #6: "Disagreements are a sign of a disintegrating marriage."

So far we have seen that many marital conflicts are the result of two very different people, with very different values, created with very different needs, trying to exist under the same roof. It should be no surprise then that most couples fight—and fight regularly.

The question is not whether we will have disagreements in our marriage, but how we will handle those conflicts. Ephesians 4:25-32 contains some helpful ground rules for fights.

1. OUR DISAGREEMENTS SHOULD BE BASED ON TRUTH. Paul began his discussion by saying, "Therefore, laying aside falsehood, speak truth, each one of you, with his neighbor, for we are members of one another" (Eph. 4:25).

Arguments that begin with "You never . . ." or "You always . . ." are usually not based on truth, but on a distortion of the truth. Rarely do husbands "never do anything to help around the house." Few wives are "always complaining." When you disagree with your spouse, don't twist, add to, or delete all of the facts. Speak honestly with your mate.

2. OUR DISAGREEMENTS SHOULD BE QUICKLY RESOLVED. Paul continued: "Be angry, and yet do not sin; do not let the sun go down on your anger" (4:26). The passage suggests that anger is inevitable, but it need not linger through the night. Make peace with your spouse before you go to sleep. Such a resolution may involve a compromise, or admitting that you were wrong, or simply agreeing to disagree. Before you retire, however, make sure your mate knows that you love him or her.

3. OUR DISAGREEMENTS SHOULD NOT DESTROY OUR MATE'S SELF-ESTEEM. Look carefully at this warning: "Let no unwholesome word proceed from your mouth, but only such a word as is good for edification according to the need of the moment, that it may give grace to those who hear. . . . Let all bitterness and wrath and anger and clamor and slander be put away from you, along with all malice" (4:29, 31).

Regardless of how much we may disagree with our mate, we should never resort to using hurtful insults that destroy our spouse's self-esteem. Comments about our spouse's appearance, character, or other sensitive areas should never be made in order to "win" an argument.

I remember reading an interview with former talk-show host Johnny Carson in which the interviewer asked what he most regretted about his job. "I suppose one regret I have is some of the things I have said on the air. I hadn't planned to say them; they just slipped out. I would give anything if I could retrieve some of those words." We need to remember that we will never be able to retrieve those words spoken to our spouse.

Myth #7: "If my spouse divorces me, it must be my fault."

We will discuss what the Bible says about divorce and remarriage a little later. But in this section we are discussing sources of unnecessary guilt. And one of those sources is guilt over an unavoidable divorce. I firmly believe that God's plan for marriage is one man with one woman for life. But what happens if a spouse chooses to have an affair or deserts the other? Listen to some Christian "experts," and they will infer that *you* are the reason for the problem. Look at what one noted Christian writer suggests you do if your spouse is having an affair:

What to Do If Your Mate Is Having an Affair

Make your home a haven, not a hassle. You may need to seriously evaluate if you have taken your relationship with your spouse for granted.

Nurture your "attraction quotient." Don't wear grubbies around the house. Lose a few pounds, smile, be warm. Be an invitation for him/her to come home to.

Take a hard look at your schedule. You may not be meeting your mate's needs because you're exhausted from a job that is too demanding. Determine where you want to succeed—at work or at home.

Offer your mate a real relationship—with real forgiveness, real love, affirmation, and encouragement. Become a magnet to draw your mate back home.[7]

Let me give you my translation of this "advice." "The reason your mate is having an affair is because you are such a fat, unattractive, nagging shrew. If you would just get your act together, maybe your spouse would not be attracted to someone else. Who can blame him/her?"

I know that is not what the author meant (I hope), but such counsel makes the deserted spouse feel unnecessarily guilty. I remember hearing a well-known seminar leader make this comment about divorce: "There is no such thing as an 'innocent party' in a divorce." I disagree. The basic reason a spouse has an affair or deserts his or her mate is because he or she has chosen to sin against God. Let's quit piling unnecessary guilt on the already sagging shoulders of those who have been the victims of adultery or desertion.

The thesis of this book has been that the way to enjoy a guilt-free existence is to reject the unrealistic expectations of others (as well as of ourselves) and to follow God's simple guidelines for each life area. The bulk of this chapter has been devoted to exploding the myths about marriage that create so much unnecessary guilt for Christian couples. But it is equally important for us to understand and obey God's requirements in marriage.

FOUR ESSENTIALS FOR A GUILT-FREE MARRIAGE

Essential #1: Marriage to a believer

Authors Bill and Lynne Hybels call this "the most unpopular requirement for marriage."[8] And yet, it is the most basic. Search the Scriptures, and you will find that God's Word is consistently clear on this subject: Believers are to only marry other believers.

Furthermore, you shall not intermarry with them; you shall not give your daughters to their sons, nor shall you take their daughters for your sons. For they will turn your sons away from following Me to serve other gods; then the anger of the Lord will be kindled against you, and He will quickly destroy you. (Deut. 7:3-4)

Now King Solomon loved many foreign women along with the daughter of Pharaoh . . . from the nations concerning which the Lord had said to the sons of Israel, "You shall not associate with them, neither shall they associate with you, for they will surely turn your heart away after their gods." Solomon held fast to these in love. . . . For it came about when Solomon was old, his wives turned his heart away after other gods; and his heart was not wholly devoted to the Lord his God, as the heart of David his father had been. (1 Kings 11:1-2, 4)

Judah has dealt treacherously, and an abomination has been committed in Israel and in Jerusalem; for Judah has profaned the sanctuary of the Lord which He loves, and has married the daughter of a foreign god. As for the man who does this, may the Lord cut off from the tents of Jacob everyone who awakes and answers, or who presents an offering to the Lord of hosts. (Mal. 2:11-12)

Do not be bound together with unbelievers; for what partnership have righteousness and lawlessness, or what fellowship has light with darkness? (2 Cor. 6:14)

I want you to notice the two reasons God prohibits marriage to unbelievers. The first involves our relationship with God. Marriage to an unbeliever breaks our fellowship with God—

not in a theological sense, but in a practical sense. When we are emotionally bound together with an unbeliever, it drags us away from our devotion to God. It happened to Solomon, it happened to the children of Israel, and it will happen to us.

Many times a young woman or man will say to me, "Pastor, I love this person so much, and maybe by dating him (her) I can win him (her) to Christ." It's a noble thought, but in the Bible there is no allowance for missionary dating!

When I was in the seventh grade, I became friends with a girl who had just moved to our city. We were good pals throughout junior high school. When we entered the ninth grade, I became concerned about the type of people she was running around with—in those days we called them "hoods." And from comments she would make in class, I knew she was not a believer. I began to pray for her and invite her to functions at my church. Eventually I had the opportunity to lead her to faith in Christ. And then I began to date her. And finally, I married her. But had I reversed the process, there is no guarantee that she would have ever become a Christian or that I would still be involved in ministry.

Marriage to an unbeliever not only can break our relationship with God; it can also fracture our relationship with our spouse. Paul asked a probing question in 2 Corinthians 6:14: "What fellowship has light with darkness?" What do light and darkness have in common? Nothing. They are opposite. One displaces the other. Enter a dark room and turn on the light—and the darkness disappears. Light and darkness cannot coexist.

That is what Paul was saying about a marriage. If the spiritual component of our lives is the most important and lasting aspect of our being, how could we ever hope to develop intimacy with a mate with whom we could not share that part of our lives? In the spiritual realm, opposites do not attract—they repel.

If I were to single out the number one cause of marital

conflict—and resulting guilt—it would be this one: the union of two spiritually incompatible people. One spouse is sold out to following Christ; the other could not care less. Imagine what would happen if two carpenters tried to build a home from two different sets of blueprints. They would experience endless arguments and frustration. And the final product would be a disaster. So it is with those couples who are trying to build a marriage without a common foundation.

Essential #2: Fidelity in your relationship
In the above paragraphs, I mentioned the major source of *conflict* in marriage—spiritual incompatibility. I believe the primary source of *guilt* in marriage is sexual immorality. In their book *The Day America Told the Truth*, authors James Patterson and Peter Kim claim that about one-third of all married Americans "have had or are now having an affair. This isn't a number from Hollywood or New York City. It's the national average for adultery. The affairs aren't one-night stands either. American affairs last, on the average, almost a year."[9] It is impossible to enjoy a guilt-free marriage without the essential ingredient of faithfulness. I doubt I even need to remind you of the biblical mandate against adultery (Exod. 20:14). Why is God so opposed to sexual relationships outside of marriage?

I recently purchased a new television set. Although it came with an instruction book, who needed to read a book to hook up a few wires? Several *hours* later, after trying every possible combination of wiring the television, cable box, and VCR, I surrendered and opened the book. To my chagrin, I found a simple diagram that showed everything I needed to know. In five minutes I had completed the job.

God's laws are like an instruction book. Because God made us, he knows what is best for us. Just as I can ignore the manufacturer's guide and plug my television into a 220-volt outlet, I can choose to ignore God's rules about sexual fidelity. In both cases the results are disastrous.

God has wired us in such a way that we need the security of the marriage relationship to be able to fully and freely enjoy our sexuality. To ignore God's command is to invite destruction into our personal lives and our marriage. In his weekly newsletter, my friend Chuck Swindoll listed some of the practical consequences of adultery:

- The total devastation it will bring to your children. Their growth, innocence, trust and healthy outlook on life will be permanently damaged.
- The embarrassment of facing other Christians, who once appreciated you, respected you, and trusted you, will be overwhelming.
- If you are engaged in the Lord's work, you will suffer the immediate loss of your job and the support of those with whom you work. The dark shadow will accompany you everywhere . . . and forever.
- Disillusionment and anger will spread rapidly among those to whom you once ministered.
- Your fall will give others license to do the same.
- Your mate will immediately be isolated by most of those who once stood near. Guilt, shame, and rejection he or she is sure to feel will accompany the anguish of loneliness.
- The inner peace you enjoyed will be gone.
- You will set in motion a generational chain reaction. You won't be able to stop it, no matter how hard you try.
- The heartache you will cause to your parents, your family, your peers, your mentors, and your disciples will be indescribable.
- You will never be able to erase the fall from your (or

others') mind. As Solomon wrote, your "reproach will not be blotted out." This will remain indelibly etched on your life's record.

- The name of Jesus Christ, whom you once honored, will be tarnished, giving the enemies of the faith further reason to sneer and jeer.
- Your mate will feel betrayed and can never again say that you are a model of fidelity. Suspicions will rob her or him of trust.
- Your escapade(s) will introduce to your life and your mate's life the very real probability of sexually transmitted disease.

I imagine some of you are rechecking the title of this book at this point. This doesn't sound like *Guilt-Free Living*. What a load to lay on someone! But don't forget that the key to guilt-free living is obedience to God's requirements. Violation of those requirements will result in real guilt.

Swindoll closes his article with these words. "Solomon was right, 'The way of the transgressor is hard.' Forgiveness may come. The affair(s) may end. Restoration to fellowship may occur. But these consequences will not go away."[10]

Essential #3: A commitment to remain together

The third requirement for a guilt-free marriage is a commitment to stay together. This is not the place to discuss the biblical teaching on divorce and remarriage, for numerous Christian books have addressed that subject at length. But before you think I have taken the easy way out, let me summarize what I believe the biblical teaching on divorce is in three easy points:

1. God hates divorce (Mal. 2:16).
2. The Bible only makes two allowances for divorce:

adultery by a spouse or desertion (see Matt. 19:9; 1 Cor. 7:12-15).

3. Even in those cases, God desires reconciliation (read the Old Testament book of Hosea).

I want to deal with *why* God hates divorce. Some might say because divorce represents a broken vow before the Lord (see Ecclesiastes 5:4-6). That is certainly true. Others might reason that unfaithfulness to one's mate is symptomatic of unfaithfulness to God. Probably. But I believe the main reason God hates divorce is because of what it does to us and to those around us.

Someone has said that two processes should never be entered into prematurely: embalming and divorcing one's mate. Actually those two processes have a lot in common: They both involve death. Divorce does not just represent the death of a marriage; it symbolizes the emotional death of two individuals.

Author Pat Conroy describes the emotional trauma of his own divorce:

> For a year I walked around feeling as if I had undergone a lobotomy. There were records I could not listen to because of their association with Barbara, poems I could not read from books I could not pick up. There is a restaurant I will never return to because it was the scene of an angry argument between us. It was a year when memory was an acid. I began to develop the odd habits of the very lonely. I turned the stereo on as soon as I entered my apartment. I drank to the point of not caring. I cooked elaborate meals for myself, then could not eat them. I had entered into the dark country of divorce, and for a year I was one of its ruined citizens.[11]

Unfortunately, the emotional trauma of divorce does not end with the husband and wife but extends to children and grandchildren. Dr. Armand Nicholi, a psychiatrist at Harvard University Medical School and Massachusetts General Hospital, cites one study in which 90 percent of the children from divorced homes suffered from a severe sense of shock when their parents separated. One-third of the children feared abandonment by the other parent. Fifty percent of the boys and girls felt abandoned and rejected. Five years later, 37 percent of the children were more unhappy than after the first eighteen months.[12]

But no statistics can describe the lasting effect of divorce on a child more than the following letter, quoted in Dr. James Dobson's book *Straight Talk to Men and Their Wives*. In the letter, a fourteen-year-old girl describes the emotional trauma of seeing her father desert the family:

> When I was ten, my parents got a divorce. Naturally, my father told me about it, because he was my favorite.
>
> "Honey, I know it's been kind of bad for you these last few days, and I don't want to make it worse. But there's something I have to tell you. Honey, your mother and I got a divorce."
>
> "But, Daddy—"
>
> "I know you don't want this, but it has to be done. Your mother and I just don't get along like we used to. I'm already packed and my plane is leaving in half an hour."
>
> "But, Daddy, why do you have to leave?"
>
> "Well, honey, your mother and I can't live together anymore."
>
> "I know that, but I mean why do you have to leave town?"
>
> "Oh. Well, I got someone waiting for me in New Jersey."
>
> "But, Daddy, will I ever see you again?"
>
> "Sure you will, honey. We'll work something out."

"But what? I mean, you'll be living in New Jersey, and I'll be living here in Washington."

"Maybe your mother will agree to your spending two weeks in the summer and two in the winter with me."

"Why not more often?"

"I don't think she'll agree to you spending two weeks in the summer and two in the winter, much less more."

"Well, it can't hurt to try."

"I know, honey, but we'll have to work it out later. My plane leaves in twenty minutes and I've got to get to the airport. Now I'm going to get my luggage, and I want you to go to your room so you don't have to watch me. And no long good-byes either."

"OK, Daddy. Good-bye. Don't forget to write."

"I won't. Good-bye. Now go to your room."

"OK. Daddy, I don't want you to go!"

"I know, honey. But I have to."

"Why?"

"You wouldn't understand, honey."

"Yes, I would."

"No, you wouldn't."

"Oh well. Good-bye."

"Good-bye. Now go to your room. Hurry up."

"OK. Well, I guess that's the way life goes sometimes."

"Yes, honey. That's the way life goes sometimes."

After my father walked out that door, I never heard from him again.[13]

I doubt that father will ever enjoy a guilt-free life.

Essential #4: Sacrificial love

A fourth ingredient for a guilt-free marriage is an unconditional love for our spouse. At the beginning of the weddings I conduct,

I always make this statement: "Marriage was instituted by God as a human object lesson of a divine truth: that Jesus Christ laid down his life for the church. Thus, more than anything, your marriage is to be an illustration of the love and forgiveness available from Christ Jesus."

This idea of marriage illustrating Christ's love for us is hardly original. In Ephesians 5:25 and 28, Paul wrote, "Husbands, love your wives, just as Christ also loved the church and gave Himself up for her. . . . So husbands ought also to love their own wives as their own bodies."

How do I demonstrate my unconditional love for my spouse and thus be able to enjoy a guilt-free marriage?

1. THROUGH ACTS OF KINDNESS. In 1 Corinthians 13:4, Paul described love as being "kind." The Greek word translated "kind" means "useful, serving, gracious." When is the last time you did something useful or kind for your spouse, not because you wanted something in return, but out of love and appreciation for him or her? Can you recall the last time you offered to take the kids for a few hours so that your spouse could relax? Or have you ever written your spouse a note of appreciation for all he or she means to you?

A few years ago, my wife had run up an extra large amount on her charge card. She was diligently working to pay off the balance, using her money from a part-time teaching job to pay off the debt. I could see that her debt was causing her unnecessary anxiety. One evening I came home and told her not to worry about the credit card balance any longer. I would take care of it. I will never forget the look of relief on her face. She still talks about what an "unexpected" and "kind" thing it was for me to do.

God demonstrated that same kindness to us. Titus 3:4-5 states that "when the kindness of God our Savior and His love for mankind appeared, He saved us, not on the basis of deeds which we have done in righteousness, but according to His mercy." When we least deserved it, God did the kindest and most useful thing of all. He sent Christ to die for us.

2. THROUGH FORGIVENESS. In 1 Corinthians 13:5 Paul gave another manifestation of unconditional love: "[Love] does not take into account a wrong suffered." The New International Version says love "keeps no record of wrongs." The Greek word used here, *logizomai*, refers to an account ledger recording debits and credits. Unfortunately, many husbands and wives keep an active ledger in which any credits (like the one I earned with my wife for the paid-off credit card bill) are offset by debits.

Recently a couple was in my office for counseling. The husband was guilty of an extramarital affair and gave every evidence of repentance. When I asked the wife if she would make the choice to forgive her mate, she groused, "I may forgive you, but I will never forget." What she was really saying was that she would simply file his offense away until it is needed!

Such a relationship will never survive. Forgiveness is the lubricant that keeps marriages running smoothly. Why should we forgive our spouse? Not because they deserve it, but because of what Christ has done for us. In Romans 4:8, Paul paraphrased Psalm 32:2: "Blessed is the man whose sin the Lord will not take into account." The word again is *logizomai*. God keeps no ledger of our wrongs; why should we keep a record of others' offenses?

The best evidence that we have truly received God's forgiveness in our lives is our willingness to forgive others—including our spouse—of their offenses against us. Paul wrote the best prescription for expressing unconditional love to our spouse: "And be kind to one another, tender-hearted, *forgiving* each other, just as God in Christ also has forgiven you" (Eph. 4:32, emphasis mine). That is the essence of sacrificial love.

Psychologist Larry Crabb says that humans have two basic emotional needs: (1) the security of being truly loved and accepted and (2) the significance of making a substantial, lasting, positive impact on another person.[14] Both of those needs can be fully satisfied by following God's simple principles for a guilt-free marriage.

The only subject more discussed (and therefore more prone to produce guilt) in the Christian community than marriage is the focus of our next chapter.

. . . . .

CHAPTER 8

Guilt-Free Parenting

A S I write these words, I am in the midst of a riot in our church—pardon me if I seem a little distracted. The cause of the riot? Chuck Swindoll, one of America's foremost authorities on the Christian home, is coming to our church tomorrow night. And our church members have gone crazy!

It all started last week when I made the simple announcement that because of the capacity crowd we expected, only adults would be allowed in the auditorium to hear Chuck's message. We would have alternative plans for the children and teenagers. Well, that did it! You have never heard such words of indignation from some of our parents:

"I can't believe you are calling this a 'family rally' and won't let me sit with my kids."

"Why does the church want to separate me from my children?" (Never mind the fact that these same parents do all they can the rest of the week to get away from their kids!)

"My child *must* hear Chuck. Our family is coming apart!"

Our staff is so concerned with the frenzied atmosphere developing for the rally tomorrow night, we have hired three security guards just to keep people from rushing Chuck to "touch the hem of his garment." It's crazy!!

I don't think our church is unique. Announce a seminar on the family, and it will be packed out. Write a book on the family, and it is almost guaranteed to be a best-seller. Preach a sermon on parenting, and it will be the most requested tape of the year. Why?

I think many of us carry around a load of guilt about our parenting skills that makes us yearn for any source of promised relief. Some of the guilt we feel is legitimate. Much is illegitimate. Like the subject of marriage, Christian parenting has become a cottage industry for publishers, preachers, and radio programs. The result has been a mixed blessing.

On one hand, many parents have been helped and challenged with insights that guide them through the seemingly impossible challenge of parenting. Yet the downside of the flood of information about parenting is that the myth of the *ideal Christian parent* has been created—a myth impossible for anyone to fulfill. Read enough books or listen to enough sermons about Christian parenting, and you will discover that the *ideal Christian parent:*

- Begins the day by having a family devotion with his/her children before they go to school (The really spiritual parents don't send children to school—they home school.)
- Sets aside an hour during the day to pray for his children
- Spends a minimum of five nights a week at home with his children
- Refuses to allow his children to watch television; in-

stead, plans exhilarating and innovative projects for his
children each evening after dinner
- Limits his children's music to George Beverly Shea
and/or Dino
- Prohibits his children to date until they are twenty-
one (and then only with an escort) . . . and on and on

One Christian father expressed the frustration and guilt he
feels this way:

> I'm so weary of all the images. At church I'm supposed to
> be some sort of a bionic Christian. At work, I'm supposed
> to be some kind of robot. And now at home, I'm expected
> to be some sort of a Christian Super Dad. It's no wonder
> that I feel like a failure most of the time. What confuses
> me is that I thought Christianity was supposed to set us
> free, instead of tying us up in new knots all the time with
> impossible expectations.[1]

THE RESPONSIBILITIES OF A CHRISTIAN PARENT

In this chapter we are going to attempt to loosen the knots of
unrealistic expectations that are strangling so many parents
with guilt. The best way to destroy those unrealistic expectations is to look at what the Bible says are our basic responsibilities as a Christian parent. Right now, forget everything that
you have heard, and see what God's Word says is your responsibility as a parent.

1. Dedicate your child to God.

I had only been at my present church a few Sundays when I was
told that we had a parents dedication scheduled for the end of
our service. At the appropriate time I recognized our gifted
preschool director, who called the parents forward, each

mother proudly carrying her infant. After they were all in a semicircle around the platform, I made a few remarks about the importance of dedicating our children to the Lord and then offered a dedicatory prayer.

After the service a member approached me and told me in no uncertain terms that I had goofed. "This is not a baby dedication, it is a *parents* dedication. You cannot dedicate a child (or anyone else) to God. Parents only can dedicate themselves to the task of raising a child."

I smiled and thanked the woman for her insight—remember, I was new to the church. But inwardly I knew she was wrong. As an infant, my parents had dedicated me to the Lord (in an Assembly of God church, of all places! I thought about sharing that with my Southern Baptist parishioner—but I knew it would be too much for her to handle!).

But beyond my own experience, I know that the dedication of our children to the Lord is a biblical principle. The story of Hannah and her son Samuel provides a beautiful illustration of what it means to dedicate our children to the Lord. You will remember that Hannah, the barren wife of Elkanah, had wept bitterly before God because of her inability to conceive. Each year she traveled with her husband to Shiloh, where they would worship God and offer their sacrifices. On one occasion, Hannah was so overcome with grief over her childlessness that she prayed:

> O Lord of hosts, if Thou wilt indeed look on the affliction of Thy maidservant and remember me, and not forget Thy maidservant, but wilt give Thy maidservant a son, then I will give him to the Lord all the days of his life, and a razor shall never come on his head. (1 Sam. 1:11)

When the Lord allowed Hannah to conceive a son, whom

she named Samuel (meaning in Hebrew "asked of the Lord"), she remembered her promise to God. When Samuel was old enough to be weaned from her, Hannah delivered her toddler to Eli the priest.

She said to Eli, "For this boy I prayed, and the Lord has given me my petition. . . . So I have also dedicated him to the Lord; as long as he lives he is dedicated to the Lord" (1 Sam. 1:27-28).

Every time I read this story I am amazed at Hannah's sacrifice. Just imagine all the "firsts" she missed by seeing her preschooler only once a year: his first words, his first day at school, his first toys, his first friends. She missed all of these things voluntarily. Why?

Hannah realized that Samuel, like all children, was simply on loan from God to his parents. God had a unique purpose for Samuel's life. Hannah was only one instrument God would use to help Samuel realize his eternal purpose in life.

Do we see your child as just being on loan to you from God? Do you understand that he has a unique plan for that toddler or grade-schooler or teenager in your home? Have you come to grips with the fact that you are only one of *many* tools God will use to accomplish his purpose in your child's life?

To dedicate our child to God means to give our child completely to God. No, we do not have to drop them off on the doorstep of the church and let the pastor and deacons raise them. But we must be willing to give up *our* dreams, desires, and aspirations for our children so that they may realize *God's* plans for their lives.

2. Encourage your child to become a Christian.

Nothing is more painful as parents than seeing our children suffer. You know the feeling you have when a child is sick or suffering—from a broken bone or from the hurt of a friend. At those times you wish you could endure the hurt in place of your child.

But as you look across the breakfast table at the children God has given you, do you realize that they are headed for an eternity of suffering in hell unless they have made the deliberate choice to become Christians? Hell is not the product of some evangelist's overactive imagination. Hell is a reality. Jesus taught that it was a place of eternal suffering (Matt. 13:42). And more disturbing is the warning Jesus gave that more people will go to hell than to heaven (Matt. 7:13-14).

How can you encourage your child to escape the reality of hell and to begin an eternal relationship with God? My first suggestion is to *pray for your child daily.* Before my first daughter was born, I began praying that she would become a Christian early in life. I don't begin to understand how predestination and God's sovereignty affect the salvation of anyone, including my child. But I believe that our prayers move the hand of God—especially in the lives of our children.

When Hannah delivered Samuel to Eli and the priests at Shiloh, the Bible tells us that "Samuel did not yet know the Lord, nor had the word of the Lord yet been revealed to him" (1 Sam. 3:7). But Hannah prayed intensely for her son, and the result was that "the Lord revealed Himself to Samuel at Shiloh by the word of the Lord" (3:21).

Next, I suggest that you *realize that becoming a Christian is a natural response for your child.* So many parents I deal with as a pastor cannot believe that their child is mature enough to become a Christian. "You mean this kid that can't even make it to the bathroom on time is ready to make a life-changing, eternal decision?" It's a natural concern but one that is predicated on a basic misconception. Many parents have the mistaken idea that children need to be more like adults in order to become believers. But Jesus said adults need to become more like children: "Truly I say to you, unless you are converted and become like children, you shall not enter the kingdom of heaven. Whoever then humbles himself as this child, he is the greatest in the kingdom of heaven. And whoever receives one such child in My name receives Me" (Matt. 18:3-5).

I remember hearing the statistic that 86 percent of Christians were saved before the age of fifteen. Matthew Henry was saved at age eleven. Jonathan Edwards was converted when he was seven. The great evangelist D. L. Moody, who was saved later in life but dedicated his early ministry to children, said, "If children are old enough to come to Sunday school, they are old enough to come to Calvary." The fact is that most children are more willing to admit their sin and their need for a Savior than most adults.

Third, *impress upon your child the importance of trusting in Christ*. The natural course of life will give you many opportunities to talk about eternal issues with your child. The death of a relative, the salvation of one of your child's friends, your own child's misbehavior, the worship services of the church, and the natural questions your child may ask all give you a perfect opportunity to talk to your child about Christ.

Every night before she went to bed, I talked to my daughter Julia about eternal issues and answered many questions she had. For several years I would say to her every night, "Julia, the most important decision you will ever make is to become a Christian. I am praying that when you are ready, you will do that." I never pressured her, but she understood what an important issue salvation was.

Finally, when you sense that your child is ready to become a Christian, *make a special appointment with your child to explain the gospel and to lead him or her to trust in Christ*. Your child needs to be able to look back at a specific time when he or she prayed to become a Christian. That time needs to be so special that it makes a lasting impression upon your child.

When she was five years old, Julia told her mom during the invitation time of our worship service that she was ready to become a Christian. My wife, Amy, explained that she first needed to talk with me. So I scheduled an appointment the next day with my five-year-old daughter. She came into my office and climbed into the large wing chair across from me. She had rarely been in my office, so she sensed this was something important. I talked with her about what it means to become a Christian, made sure that she had an understanding of her own sin and what Christ had done for her, and then I led her in a prayer to trust in Christ. After our prayer, I hugged her and congratulated her on becoming a Christian. It has now been several years since that experience, but she always refers to her conversion as the time she "came to Daddy's office." It made an impression on her that this was a life-changing decision.

I once thought that the thrill of being in the delivery room, seeing my two children born, was the greatest joy imaginable. But that pales in comparison to the satisfaction of leading my children to faith in Christ and knowing that I will spend eternity with them in heaven.

3. Communicate spiritual values to your child.
Our responsibility for the spiritual well-being of our children does not end with their conversion. We have a responsibility to communicate spiritual truth to our children throughout their lives. Moses' final words to the Israelites as they prepared to enter the Promised Land provide a model of communication of such truth.

Moses warned the Israelites that they would face numerous temptations in the new land. The immorality of the Canaanites they would witness, the variety of false religions they would encounter, and the prosperity they would enjoy would tempt the Israelites to turn away from serving the true God.

> Hear, O Israel! The Lord is our God, the Lord is one! And you shall love the Lord your God with all your heart and with all your soul and with all your might. And these words, which I am commanding you today, shall be on your heart; and you shall teach them diligently to your sons and shall talk of them when you sit in your house and when you walk by the way and when you lie down and when you rise up. (Deut. 6:4-7)

Moses explained that the spiritual survival of the nation depended on the adults' fidelity to God *and* upon their willingness to communicate those same values to their children. I am impressed by several truths from these few verses about communicating spiritual values to children.

First, *communicating spiritual values to children requires authenticity.* Parents cannot pass on to their children what they do not possess themselves. Moses told parents that God's commands must first "be on your heart." Christian psychologists Paul and Richard Meier tell the following story:

> Jack M. was a forty-five-year-old father who was being treated in our psychiatry ward for alcoholism. During a group therapy session Mr. M. avoided discussing his own problems by bragging to the group about what a good disciplinarian he was with his children. He told us that he made his children go to church every Sunday morning, Sunday night, and Wednesday night. When a group member asked him if he went with them, he replied, "Well, no, I don't, because I'm too restless and can't sit still that long." Then he bragged about how he made his children

study their schoolwork for one hour every night and also read their Bible every night. I asked him if he studied very much or read his Bible every day. He replied, "Well, no, I don't because I get bored too easy when I read." Mr. M. still went on to brag that he didn't let his children watch any television whatsoever. When a group member asked him why, he replied, "Because there's too many beer commercials on TV." I asked him what he had been doing every night for the past few years, and he finally admitted, "I've been sitting at home watching television every night and drinking about a fifth of whiskey."

He was offended that we made him aware of the fact that he was setting a poor example for his children. His children will probably turn out the very opposite of what he wants, because he is telling them one thing and practicing another.[2]

Until our children learn by our example that there is nothing more important in life than loving and serving God, our words will seem hollow.

Second, I notice that *communicating spiritual truth to children requires intense effort.* Moses says that we are to teach our children "diligently." That is, we are to realize the urgency of communicating spiritual values to our children. Moses was talking to the Israelites as they prepared to enter a pagan country. He understood that they were entering a country that was opposed to the principles of God's Word. Their only chance of success as a nation was to obey God's laws themselves and pass on those laws to succeeding generations.

In the same way, if you are trying to raise godly children today, you are swimming against the tide. Your children are being bombarded with ideas and values that are contrary to the

Christian faith. The task is urgent. One writer expressed it this way:

> The prize is the inner spirit of my children and the stakes are high. Arrayed against me are those who wish to extract money, loyalty, and the strong creative energy my son or daughter may have to give. In the eternal dimension, the prize is the soul of my children. I am not prepared to compromise or negotiate. Until my children are old and wise enough to distinguish their enemies from their friends, I hold the responsibility to conduct both a defense and offense on their behalf.[3]

Finally, *communicating spiritual values to children requires consistency.* We don't teach our children the importance of loving and obeying God by pulling out the family Bible once a week (or even once a day) and lecturing on "one hundred reasons we can believe in the Virgin Birth of Christ." Instead, the most effective teaching comes out of the natural flow of family life: when we sit around the table for a meal, when we travel in the car, when we watch television, before we say good night, when we get up in the morning. Again, the natural circumstances of life (family crises, current events, circumstances with friends, or problems at school) will give us many opportunities to illustrate the consequences of obeying or disobeying God.

Without such instruction, our children are destined to become conformed to the values of the prevailing culture. Author Thomas Merton writes:

> The modern child may early in his or her existence have natural inclinations toward spirituality. The child may have imagination, originality, a simple and individual response to reality and even a tendency to moments of

thoughtful silence and absorption. All these tendencies, however, are soon destroyed by the dominant culture. The child becomes a yelling, brash, false little monster, brandishing a toy gun, or dressed up like some character he has seen on television. His head is filled with inane slogans, songs, noises, explosions, statistics, brand names, menaces, and clichés. Then, when the child gets to school, he learns to verbalize, rationalize, to pace, to make faces like an advertisement, to need a car, and in short, to go through life with an empty head conforming to others like himself, in togetherness.[4]

The goal in communicating spiritual truth to our children is for them to embrace those truths, rather than to allow the culture to squeeze our children into its mold.

4. Discipline your child.
An attempt to address the subject of discipline in a few paragraphs seems superficial at best. Many excellent books are available on this subject. The purpose of this chapter is to alleviate much of the guilt parents feel about parenting by outlining the few basic principles God's Word gives about this subject. And one of those basic responsibilities God gives every parent is to discipline his children. Just look at some of the many passages in Scripture dealing with discipline:

> If any man has a stubborn and rebellious son who will not obey his father or his mother, and when they chastise him, he will not even listen to them, then his father and mother shall seize him, and bring him out to the elders of his city at the gateway of his home town. And they shall say to the elders of his city, "This son of ours is stubborn and rebellious, he will not obey us, he is a glutton and a drunkard."

Then all the men of his city shall stone him to death; so you shall remove the evil from your midst, and all Israel shall hear of it and fear. (Deut. 21:18-21)

My son, do not reject the discipline of the Lord, or loathe His reproof, for whom the Lord loves He reproves, even as a father, the son in whom he delights. (Prov. 3:11-12)

A wise son accepts his father's discipline, but a scoffer does not listen to rebuke. (Prov. 13:1)

He who spares his rod hates his son, but he who loves him disciplines him diligently. (Prov. 13:24)

A fool rejects his father's discipline, but he who regards reproof is prudent. (Prov. 15:5)

Discipline your son while there is hope, and do not desire his death. (Prov. 19:18)

Stripes that wound scour away evil, and strokes reach the innermost parts. (Prov. 20:30)

Train up a child in the way he should go, even when he is old he will not depart from it. (Prov. 22:6)

Do not hold back discipline from the child, although you beat him with the rod, he will not die. You shall beat him with the rod, and deliver his soul from Sheol. (Prov. 23:13-14)

As I read through these passages and others about discipline, several principles emerge.

1. DISCIPLINE IS A DEMONSTRATION OF OUR LOVE FOR OUR CHILD. If you truly love your child, you will discipline him. The writer of Hebrews, in discussing God's discipline in our lives, quoted Proverbs 3:11-12 (see above) and then added his own comment: "But if you are without discipline, of which all have become partakers, then you are illegitimate children and not sons" (Heb. 12:8). The writer was saying that the signal proof we belong to God is that he corrects us when we sin. A parent who allows his child to play in the street, stick his finger into an electrical outlet, or play with a loaded gun is a negligent parent. Likewise, a parent who refuses to correct his child who breaks God's laws is also negligent.

In his landmark book *Dare to Discipline*, James Dobson writes:

> The parent must convince himself that punishment . . . is not something that he does *to* the child; it is something he does *for* the child. His attitude toward his disobedient youngster is this, "I love you too much to let you behave like that."[5]

2. DISCIPLINE SHOULD BEGIN EARLY IN YOUR CHILD'S LIFE. The phrase "spare the rod, spoil the child" is built on the first phrase of Proverbs 13:24—"He who spares his rod hates his son." But the second part of that verse is equally important: "But he who loves him disciplines him diligently." The word translated "diligently" originally meant "early dawn." Solomon is not advising you to wake your child before the sun rises to punish him. He is talking about starting the process of correction early in a child's life.

In his book *Seeds of Greatness*, Denis Waitley illustrates the dangers of waiting too long to begin the process of discipline with a section he titles "Bradford the Barbarian":

In my parenting and leadership seminars, I tell a true story about a young couple who invited me to their home for dinner some time ago after an all-day program at a university. This man and woman, both highly intelligent, with advanced degrees, had opted for a "child-centered" home so their five-year-old son Bradford would have everything at his disposal to become a winner out there in the competitive world. When I arrived at their driveway in front of a fashionable two-story Tudor home at the end of a cul-de-sac, I should have known what was in store for me. I stepped on his E. T. doll getting out of the car and was greeted by "Watch where you're walking or you'll have to buy me a new one!"

Entering the front door, I instantly discovered that this was Bradford's place, not his parents'. The furnishings, it appeared, were originally of fine quality. I thought I recognized an Ethan Allen piece that had suffered the "wrath of Khan." We attempted to have a cup of hot cider in the family room, but Bradford was busy ruining his new Intellivision controls. Trying to find a place to sit down was like hopping on one foot through a mine field, blindfolded.

Bradford got to eat first, in the living room, so he wouldn't be lonely. I nearly dropped my hot cup in my lap in surprise when they brought out a high chair that was designed like an aircraft ejection seat with four legs and straps. (I secretly visualized a 20-millimeter cannon shell, strapped to a skyrocket under the seat, with a two-second fuse.) He was five years old, and had to be strapped in a high chair to get through one meal!

As we started our salads in the dining room, which was an open alcove adjoining the living room, young Bradford dumped his dinner on the carpet and proceeded to pour his milk on top of it to ensure that the peas and carrots would go deep into the shag fibers. His mother entreated, "Brad, honey, don't do that. Mommy wants you to grow up strong and healthy like Daddy. I'll get you some more dinner while Daddy cleans it up."

While they were occupied with their chores, Bradford had unfastened his seat belts, scrambled down from his perch, and joined me in the dining room, helping himself to my olives. "I think you should wait for your own dinner," I said politely, removing his hand from my salad bowl. He swung his leg up to kick me in the knee, but my old ex-pilot reflexes didn't fail me and I crossed my legs so quickly that he missed, came off his feet, and came down hard on the floor on the seat of his pants. You'd have thought he was at the dentist's office! He screamed and ran to his mother, sobbing, "He hit me!" When his parents asked what happened, I calmly informed them that he had fallen accidentally and that, besides, "I'd never hit the head of a household!"[6]

The Bible advises you to start disciplining your child early in life or run the risk of raising your own version of Bradford.

3. DISCIPLINE INVOLVES PAIN. Child psychologists will always debate whether or not corporal punishment is effective. But the Bible does not stutter on the issue. We have already looked at Proverbs 13:24: "He who spares his rod hates his son, but he who loves him disciplines him diligently." Consider also Proverbs 23:13-14: "Do not hold back discipline from the child, although you beat him with the rod, he will not die. You shall beat him with the rod, and deliver his soul from Sheol."

Solomon is not advocating child abuse here. In fact, he is saying that the right kind of discipline will not harm a child. Discipline should never be administered out of anger, but out of a sincere desire to deliver the child from destructive behavior that would cost him his eternal soul.

But discipline involves *more* than physical pain. You have no doubt heard the story about the boy who was ordered to sit in the corner for his misbehavior. He refused to sit down. After his mom threatened him with a spanking, he relented but muttered to himself, "I may be sitting on the outside, but I'm standing on the inside." If you only exercise physical discipline with your child, you will produce children who are "standing on the inside."

How many parents do you know who have wayward teenagers and who say, "I can't figure out what went wrong. I strictly disciplined my children when they were young." The answer is that discipline involves more than corporal punishment. In his excellent book *Know Your Child*, Joe Temple points out that in the Bible there are three Hebrew words translated "correction." The first word, *mosayraw*, refers to corporal punishment. The second word translated "correction," *yawsar*, refers to a verbal scolding. This kind of correction is mentioned in Proverbs 29:17: "Correct your son, and he will give you comfort; he will also delight your soul."

Solomon is saying that not every offense requires physical discipline. Don't feel guilty for not always spanking your child. Some transgressions are better handled through strong words than with a firm hand. However, we need to be careful to show restraint here as well. Harsh words can permanently injure a child's spirit, just as a severe beating can injure a child's body. We should be careful never to use sarcasm or cutting remarks that damage a child's fragile self-esteem.

The third word for correction in the Bible is the word *yawkah*. It is a word that relates correction to love. The emphasis is much more positive than negative. Notice how Solomon uses this word in Proverbs 3:11: "My son, do not reject the discipline of the Lord, or loathe His reproof, for whom the Lord loves He reproves, even as a father, the son in whom he delights." In his book, Temple demonstrates that this word is used throughout the Old Testament to refer to reasonable discussion, not heated arguments. Temple then relates the word to discipline with these words:

> All of this should enforce the idea that if you are going to correct your child, you should correct him with a willingness for discussion about the things for which you are correcting him. Of course, such discussion is not always necessary. Sometimes you correct your child and the child knows very well why you are correcting him. I am not suggesting that for every time you correct him you have to sit down and go over again the reason why you are correcting him. But you ought to have an open mind and an open heart, and if the child has one sincere question, you ought never to say to him, "You do it because I said so; that is why!" You have no right to say that. If you are going to correct your child as God corrects His children, you must allow time for sincere discussion.[7]

In summary, the Bible allows for different kinds of discipline, depending on the nature of the offense and the nature of your individual child. Not all offenses are alike; not all children are alike. Some respond better to verbal discipline than physical discipline. One key to guilt-free parenting is to discipline your child according to his or her individual need—not according to standardized formulas found in books and sermons.

5. Sacrifice for your child.
Another important ingredient for guilt-free parenting is making the appropriate sacrifices for our children. "Wait a minute,

Robert!" you warn. "Sounds like you are getting ready to pile on the guilt, not remove it!" Not really. I don't think anything produces more needless guilt than regret. Difficult circumstances are hard enough without feeling that *you* are the cause of your problem.

In relation to parenting, nothing is more painful than looking back and realizing that there were sacrifices you could have made for your children but didn't. Especially when the child goes astray. Let me identify three sacrifices every parent needs to make for his child.

1. TIME. We need to be careful here not to induce illegitimate guilt. Read very many Christian books, and you will see a running theme of condemnation towards mothers who work outside the home and husbands who work more than forty-hour weeks. Yes, some parents' overemphasis on material possessions is the root cause of too much time spent at work. But some parents have no choice. Some mothers must work. Some dads can't enjoy the luxury of a nine-to-five, Monday-through-Friday job.

But when we do have a choice, children need to take priority over our careers. Ann Landers writes:

> The moral fiber of family life is coming apart at the seams because there's nobody home. Parents are not spending enough time with their children. They can't. The rat race is highly competitive and children aren't valued the way they once were. Children were considered at least as important as a career. But no longer is this true. The career gets the quality time, and the kids get what's left over."[8]

Although we may not always have control over our work

schedule, we can regulate our discretionary time. Tim Kimmel, in his book *Raising Kids Who Turn Out Right*, writes:

> Who wouldn't want to come home to a quiet house, soak in the bathtub for an hour, take a little nap, prepare and enjoy a leisurely dinner? But reality dictates terms as soon as the garage door goes up. The kids are there with their needs, their questions, their worries, and their secrets . . . and they expect us to give them our best. They can't understand that we gave our best to our employer and there's nothing left to squeeze out.
>
> That's how children in good homes can end up emotional latchkey kids. Their parents are so preoccupied with their own personal needs and frustrations that they don't have time to focus on the emotional needs and frustrations of their children.
>
> The little kids want to be held, the middle-sized kids want you to play with them, and the big kids want to be talked with rather than talked to. All of these activities engage their emotions and help to stabilize their fragile emotional systems.
>
> When we parents succumb to our own needs at the expense of those of our kids, we force them to do the best they can on their own. Unfortunately, a child is not born with the intuitive skills needed to make balanced choices and draw right conclusions. Those skills are deposited in the early years by careful parents.[9]

One study has shown that fathers interact with their small children an average of thirty-seven seconds per day. Another survey among three hundred seventh- and eighth-grade boys revealed that their fathers spent a total of seven and one-half minutes alone with them.[10] To sacrifice time for your children may mean saying no to a football game, a trip to the mall, an evening out with friends, or a meeting at the church.

2. MONEY. My father worked for an airline. When I was still in the womb, he was making $440 a month. But when he discovered that my mother was pregnant with me, he used an airline pass, flew to Chicago, and spent a half a month's salary at Moody Bible Institute buying Christian books for me to read. It may sound silly. Yet he was willing to sacrifice his limited income for my benefit. I often think of that story when I read Jesus' words in Matthew 7:11: "If you then, being evil, know how to give good gifts to your children, how much more shall your Father who is in heaven give what is good to those who ask Him!"

Many times we focus on the second part of that verse—God's willingness to answer our prayers (as we will see in chapter 11). But Jesus was also teaching that it is natural for us to want to give good gifts to our children: books that will enhance their intellectual and spiritual development, an education that will prepare them for the future, medical care that will ensure a healthy life, an inheritance that will provide for their future security and their children's needs. What are you willing to sacrifice to provide those gifts: a car you've always dreamed of, an exotic vacation, a suit of clothes you saw in the catalog? Guilt-free parenting necessitates sacrificing money for the benefit of our children.

3. DREAMS. Maybe this is the hardest sacrifice of all. All of us have aspirations for our children. We have in mind a college we want them to attend, a sport in which we would like for them to participate, an instrument we think they should play, a career they should enjoy, or a mate that would meet our approval. But sometimes we must be willing to sacrifice our dreams so that we may help our child realize God's plans, his purpose for their lives. To *love* our children means to *be willing to sacrifice* our own

plans for our children—for their good and for God's eternal purpose.

6. Entrust your child to God.

I come now to the most crucial step in guilt-free parenting. We can dedicate our children to God, encourage them to become Christians, communicate spiritual values to them, discipline them, and sacrifice for them. But ultimately *they* choose the path on which they will travel. Their future in this life and their destiny in the next life are the products of their own choices.

Proverbs 22:6 states, "Train up a child in the way he should go, even when he is old he will not depart from it." That promise has been comforting to some and confusing to others. Is the verse promising our children will turn out right if we rear them correctly? If so, how do you explain godly parents who have godless children? Or, even more puzzling, how do you explain the differences among children from the same family? One serves the Lord faithfully; the other lives in rebellion.

A closer examination of this text reveals that the phrase "in the way he should go" refers to the individual tendencies of your child. In other words, we should tailor-make the training of our children according to their individual gifts, interests, and inclinations toward sin. One child may be athletic and extroverted, have a tendency toward pride, and respond only to physical discipline. Another child may be scholastic, introverted, a habitual liar, and respond to verbal correction. Obviously, you would not try to deal with these two children in the same way. That is what Solomon is saying. A wise parent trains his child according to the individual inclinations of that child, for even when the child is old, he will follow those inclinations.

While we cannot control the decisions our children ultimately make, we can clearly delineate the choices that are set before them. I think again of the example of Moses. He was an old man when his spiritual children, the Israelites, were about to enter the Promised Land. He would not be allowed to lead them, nor would he live to see the path they would ultimately choose. But in his final message to the Israelites, he reminded them that they had a choice to make:

> See, I am setting before you today a blessing and a curse: the blessing, if you listen to the commandments of the Lord your God, which I am commanding you today; and the curse, if you do not listen to the commandments of the Lord your God, but turn aside from the way which I am commanding you today, by following other gods which you have not known. (Deut. 11:26-28)

Some of you reading this chapter feel like you have blown it as a parent. You are sure you have failed, because your children have not always made the right choices. But part of the guilt you feel may be due to a misunderstanding of what successful parenting really is. Successful parenting should not be defined as controlling the choices our children make. Moses could not control the Israelites. God chose not to control us. And we cannot ultimately control our children.

Instead, the essence of successful parenting is reminding your children of the choices before them and diligently encouraging them to choose the path that leads to success. When you do that, you are on the road to experiencing guilt-free parenting.

Let's look at one more relationship in life that is the source of much illegitimate guilt among Christians.

CHAPTER 9

Guilt-Free Friendships

O NE writer has expressed an ideal friendship this way:

Oh, the comfort—the inexpressible comfort of feeling safe with a person,
   Having neither to weigh thoughts,
   Nor measure words—but pouring them
   All right out—just as they are—
   Chaff and grain together—
   Certain that a faithful hand will
   Take and sift them—
   Keep what is worth keeping—
   And with the breath of kindness
   Blow the rest away.[1]

Whenever I read those words, I want to pick up the phone immediately and call my two closest friends. No reason, no agenda. Maybe it is simply a desire to relive some of those times in which I have been able to share in confidence my dreams, doubts, and discouragements with someone I completely trusted. Few things in life are more pleasurable than pouring out one's heart to a trusted soul mate with no need to "weigh thoughts." Someone has said, "There are not many things in life so beautiful as true friendship, and there are not many things more uncommon."[2]

Such a statement may make a beautiful Hallmark card—but it does not tell the whole story. Yes, good relationships are rare, but they are also difficult. Unintentional hurt, unspoken anger, unmet needs, and unrealized expectations sometimes are a part of even the best friendships.

Furthermore, for every close friendship we have developed, we can all think of many more friendships that have not survived. Moves to another city, unresolved conflicts, change in marital status, differing interests, or any other number of factors have caused once choice relationships to disintegrate. Many times we feel guilty about those lost friendships.

In this chapter we are going to identify five problems in friendships that are prone to produce guilt—especially among Christians—and discover some ways to develop and maintain guilt-free friendships.

THE VALUE OF FRIENDSHIPS

Yes, friendships can be painful, but they are also essential for our emotional health. You no doubt have heard the story about the two porcupines, huddled together in the frozen tundra of northern Canada. Pricked by each other's quills, they quickly separated. It was not long until the unbearable temperature moved them back together. They needled each other, but they also needed each other!

But the benefits of companionship extend beyond physical warmth. I think about Solomon's words in Ecclesiastes 4. Solomon was the richest, wisest, and most powerful man in all of Israel's history, and yet, reading between the lines of Ecclesiastes, we see that he was a very lonely person.

> Then I looked again at vanity under the sun. There was a certain man without a dependent, having neither a son nor a brother, yet there was no end to all his labor. Indeed, his eyes were not satisfied with riches and he never asked, "And for whom am I laboring and depriving myself of pleasure?" This too is vanity and it is a grievous task." (Eccles. 4:7-8)

The old king was saying it is futile to work and sacrifice in life if one has no one with whom to share his or her life. Don't forget that Solomon was no cloistered monk. He had plenty of people around him—seven hundred wives, three hundred concubines, numerous children, and many loyal subjects. But he was lonely.

Maybe we can relate to that sensation, having on occasion been in a crowded room and yet felt incredibly alone. We have all sat down to talk with a friend and sensed that he or she was really not listening to us.

We have all experienced those feelings from time to time. But I believe Solomon faced them continuously. His meteoric rise to the top left him with no close friends. That realization of his loneliness led him to write the following words:

> Two are better than one because they have a good return for their labor. For if either of them falls, the one will lift up his companion. But woe to the one who falls when there is not another to lift him up. Furthermore, if two lie down together they keep warm, but how can one be warm alone? And if one can overpower him who is alone, two

can resist him. A cord of three strands is not quickly torn apart. (Eccles. 4:9-12)

Solomon pictures four specific benefits of friendship—benefits that far outweigh the pain of relationships.

Friends provide help in a crisis.

Last Sunday afternoon as I was driving home from church, I noticed a stranded car at the bottom of the access ramp. Playing the part of the Good Samaritan, I pulled over and asked the woman if I could help. As I inspected the car and saw that the front left tire was flat, I realized that my help would be limited to turning on her flashers, raising the hood, and taking her to the service station (I've had many varied experiences in life—changing a flat tire is not one of them). I asked her if there was someone I could call on my car phone. She said her husband was not home; and having just moved to our city from Germany, she had no friends who could assist her. She was stuck with me.

Yes, a flat tire is a minor crisis. But suppose she had been involved in a serious accident. Who would have been there to assist her? Solomon is saying that we all need a network of friends who are there to pick us up when we "fall"—when a job is lost, when a doctor delivers bad news, or when a mate dies.

Friends offer companionship when we feel lonely.

Solomon pictures another benefit of friendship with these words: "If two lie down together they keep warm, but how can one be warm alone?" I know this sounds a little kinky—especially coming from someone who had three hundred concubines to help him "keep warm" every night. But I don't think Solomon has sex in mind here. He is talking about the warmth that friends provide when we feel alone.

I think about two "cold" times in my life when I especially

appreciated the warmth of close friends. One was the Sunday that I preached in view of a call at my present church. As I looked out upon a sea of unknown faces, it was comforting to see my two closest friends from my previous church sitting in the second row. They had wanted to be there for this important day in my life. What a joy to see people we knew who loved and supported us!

The other time was when the doctors discovered my mother had inoperable colon cancer. During the week she spent in the hospital, friends from all over the state converged on that ICU waiting room just to sit with me and encourage me. No one said anything profound, but their silence and presence kept me warm.

In his book *The Last Thing We Talk About*, the late Joe Bayly describes a friend who provided warmth after the death of one of his children:

> I was sitting, torn by grief. Someone came and talked to me of God's dealings, of why it happened, of hope beyond the grave. He talked constantly, he said things I knew were true.
>
> I was unmoved, except to wish he'd go away. He finally did.
>
> Another came and sat beside me. He didn't talk. He didn't ask leading questions. He just sat beside me for an hour and more, listened when I said something, answered briefly, prayed simply, left.
>
> I was moved. I was comforted. I hated to see him go.[3]

Friends offer support when we are mistreated.

James wrote, "Consider it all joy, my brethren, when you encounter various trials, knowing that the testing of your faith produces endurance" (1:2-3). The word translated "encounter" could be translated "ambushed." What a perfect description of how problems come!

Did you ever watch the old Saturday morning westerns on television? I think every one of those shows must have used the same location set (as well as the same actors and horses) for the "ambush scene." You've seen it a million times. The cowboys are riding on a narrow path, bordered by steep cliffs on both sides. Then suddenly, out of nowhere, the Indians emerge with their war whoops, and it's scalp time! That's how problems attack us. They come suddenly, and they are never alone—they arrive in numbers.

My ambush came at a Wednesday night business meeting a number of years ago in a former church. A few of the deacons, discontent over not being able to control the church and the new pastor as they had done for so many years, had been stirring up dissension in the congregation. When I walked into the church that evening for what I thought would be a routine business meeting, I was surprised to see the place packed. Uh-oh. I could hear the "Indians'" war whoops. I knew the ambush was coming.

I went through the regular agenda and then uttered the words that I knew might seal my fate: "Is there any other business?" With that, the ringleader of the opposition rose to his feet and pulled out a sheet of papers detailing all of my "offenses" and closed by recommending that I be removed as pastor.

Another one of the antagonists rose to offer his support for removing the pastor. And then another chimed in. After they had their chance to speak, I asked if anyone else had something they wanted to say.

An older woman at the back of the church stood up and started to approach me. "Mrs. Osburn, do you have something you wish to say?"

"No," she said as she arrived at my side, "I just want to stand by my pastor."

One by one, my closest friends, as well as others in the congregation, came and stood on both sides of me to offer their support. When there was no more room at the front, others stood up to voice their support for me. I never had to utter one word in defense. My friends took care of it for me.

We all need friends to protect us when we are under attack. Those attacks might come from people or from adverse circumstances. But regardless of their origination, we all need people who will shield us from those attacks with words, prayers, and encouragement.

It is that kind of protection Solomon had in mind when he wrote, "And if one can overpower him who is alone, two can resist him" (Eccles. 4:12). It is easy to attack someone when they are alone, but overpowering two people is more difficult. And the only thing better than having one friend stand with us is having two: "A cord of three strands is not quickly torn apart."

As you mentally survey your close friends, ask yourself several questions. Do you have someone you would call in a crisis situation? Do you have a friend who would be willing to drop everything if he or she knew you were in trouble just to be by your side? If you were unjustly attacked, do you have friends who would automatically rise to your defense?

THE PROBLEMS WITH FRIENDSHIPS

Friendships are essential, but they can also be problematic. How can we enjoy the benefits of friendships without suffering the inevitable guilt that comes with close relationships? Let's identify five problems in friendships that produce guilt and discover the solutions to those problems.

Problem #1: "I don't have enough close friends."

As I was researching the material for this chapter, I came to an obvious conclusion. The people who write books about friendships are those who have little trouble making friends. That is natural. We talk or write about those things we excel in. After reading several books on friendship, I was depressed. *What's wrong with me that I don't have more close friendships?*

As you read the previous section, you may have thought, *I must be a real loser. I don't have* anyone *I would feel comfortable calling in times of crisis. I don't know anyone who would drop everything (or anything) to be by my side or who would rise to my defense.* The low self-esteem that so many of us feel leads to the erroneous conclusion that a lack of friends is caused by some deficiency of ours. *I am not attractive, educated, or rich. No wonder people don't swarm around me.*

However, I have come to a different conclusion. The number and depth of our friendships are functions of our individual personalities. Some people are naturally extroverts, others more introverted. All of the Dale Carnegie courses in the world cannot change our basic personalities.

One key to guilt-free friendships is to accept our individual, God-given personality differences. Those differences are often manifested in the number and depth of our relationships. Jerry White writes, "Everyone has a limited capacity for friendship and each person has a different capacity for numbers of friendships."[4] White goes on to say that most people are fortunate if they have one to six intimate friends during a lifetime.

While we may have a limited capacity for the number of deep friendships we can sustain, we all can probably increase the number of our close relationships. Additionally, we can always improve the friendships we now enjoy. In his book *Motivation to Last a Lifetime*, Ted Engstrom gives ten tips for nourishing friendships:

- Permit your friends to be themselves. Accept them as they are. Be grateful for what is there, not annoyed by what friends can't give. Accept each one's imperfections—and individuality—and don't feel threatened if their opinions and tastes sometimes differ from yours.
- Give each other space. We are entitled to our private feelings and thoughts. Friends who try to invade the inner space of one another risk destroying the relationship.
- Be ready to give and to receive. Be eager to help and be able to ask for help as well. But don't be over-demanding or let yourself be used.
- Make your advice constructive. When a friend needs to talk, listen without interruption. If advice is asked for, be positive and supportive.
- Be loyal. Loyalty is faithfulness. It means "being with" our friend in bad times as well as in good. It means honoring a confidence. It means neither disparaging a friend in his absence nor allowing others to do so.
- Give praise and encouragement. Tell your friends what you like about them, how thankful you are for their presence in your life. Delight in their talents; applaud their successes.
- Be honest. Open communication is the essence of friendship. Express your feelings, good and bad, instead of bottling up your anger or anxiety. Clearing the air helps a relationship grow. But be aware of what is better left unsaid.
- Treat friends as equals. In true friendship there is no number one, no room for showing off how smart and successful you are, for envy, for feeling superior or inferior.
- Trust your friends. We live in a messy, imperfect

world made up of imperfect people. Trust can be betrayed, but trust is essential to friendship. Make the effort to believe in the intrinsic goodness of your friends.

- Be willing to risk. One of the obstacles to a close relationship is the fear of rejection and hurt. We don't want to reveal our vulnerability. But unless we dare to love others, we condemn ourselves to a sterile life.[5]

Perhaps the apostle Paul best summed up "how to win friends and influence people" when he wrote:

> Do nothing from selfishness or empty conceit, but with humility of mind let each of you regard one another as more important than himself; do not merely look out for your own personal interests, but also for the interests of others. (Phil. 2:3-4)

It is trite but nevertheless true: The best way to have friends is to practice *being* a friend.

Problem #2: "Some of the people who used to be close friends no longer are. Our friendship has changed."

Some friendships change through any variety of uncontrollable circumstances. Distance, differing interests, changes in economic status can all contribute to a change in a relationship.

The Browns and the Henrys had been close friends for years. Ron and Jack went to school together. After graduation, they decided to start a computer software business together. The business looked as if it would succeed at first. The couples spent endless hours working together to build the business. But the company soon plateaued, and sales started to plummet. Both couples agreed that it would be wise to dissolve the company before experiencing any serious losses and pursue their own careers in the computer industry. They pledged to remain close friends.

Ron immediately found a position as vice president of marketing for a major firm. Jack, however, wasn't so successful. For months he sent out resumes with no luck. Ron tried to use his connections in the industry to land Jack a position. Nothing worked. During the period of Jack's unemployment, the two couples continued to socialize. But the relationship became strained.

Ron and his wife, aware of the Henrys' financial difficulties from unemployment, would offer to pick up the check at dinner. Sometimes the Henrys would allow them to. But they felt guilty "mooching" off their friends. Likewise, Ron and his wife felt uncomfortable initiating social outings that would only spotlight their friends' money problems. So they would invite them over for potluck suppers. But then they found themselves stifled in their conversation.

Ron could not talk about his job—which consumed 60 percent of his life—without aggravating the despair Jack felt over his unemployment. Ron's wife, Helen, could not discuss the private school their children were attending, their plans for redecorating the house, or any of the other activities related to money that were integral parts of their lives.

When the Browns learned that the Henrys were two months behind in their mortgage payments, they even offered the needed money as a gift. But the Henrys refused it. How could they accept a handout from close friends who were equal partners just eighteen months earlier?

Needless to say, the once-close relationship deteriorated over a period of time and became just another superficial friendship. Both couples felt guilty over the loss of a once intimate friendship. But neither couple knows what they could have done differently.

I doubt they could have done anything to salvage the intimacy they once enjoyed. I believe that most friendships are built on level ground. The more things we share in common with another individual—geographical location, interests, economic status, sense of humor, religious beliefs, educational background, shared experiences—the more likely we are to bond with that person.

Likewise, the more significant changes that occur in any of those areas, the more likely we are to break those bonds of friendship.

How should we deal with friendships that have changed through the unavoidable circumstances of life?

1. REFUSE TO FEEL GUILTY ABOUT THE CHANGE IN YOUR FRIENDSHIP. Whatever change has come into your life—a move to another city, a promotion, a demotion—is ultimately a part of God's sovereign plan for your life. Such changes will naturally change your relationships as well.

2. THANK GOD FOR ALL OF YOUR FRIENDSHIPS—EVEN THE ONES THAT HAVE CHANGED. I often think about several friends of mine whom I once considered my closest friends. But the circumstances of life—mainly geographical moves—changed the nature of those relationships. Yes, I miss the closeness I once enjoyed with those people. But occasionally I will pray a prayer like this: "God, thank you for bringing ———— into my life just when I needed him. Take care of him, and please provide some opportunities for us to spend time together in the future." Genuinely thanking God for friendships that may have changed has a way of reminding you that God is in control of every area of your life—including your relationships. He will continue to bring people into your life who will meet your need for companionship.

3. MAINTAIN SOME CONTACT WITH YOUR FRIENDS. A telephone call, a brief note, a cartoon that you know they might enjoy are easy ways to remain in contact with once close friends. Don't expect those contacts to instantly reestablish the intimacy you previously enjoyed. But such contacts make it easier to cope with changed relationships, rather than completely rooting those people out of your life.

Problem #3: "Some of my best friends are not believers. My Christian friends warn me not to be 'bound together with unbelievers.' Should I end those friendships with non-Christians?"

The way to enjoy a guilt-free life is to understand what the Bible says and what it doesn't say about every life area—including friendships.

Nowhere does the Bible prohibit our association with unbelievers. Possibly you have heard someone use the verse in James 4:4 to restrict relationships with non-Christians: "You adulteresses, do you not know that friendship with the world is hostility toward God? Therefore whoever wishes to be a friend of the world makes himself an enemy of God." Yet to fully understand that verse, one must clearly define the term *world*. The word *world* (*cosmos* in Greek) does not refer to people, but to a system that is opposed to the principles of God. Charles Ryrie defines *world* as "that organized system headed by Satan that leaves God out and is a rival to him. Though God loves the world of men, believers are not to love at all that which organizes them against God."[6] This verse, then, is not a prohibition of becoming friends with unbelievers, but a warning not to adopt the value system of this world that denies God and the truths of his Word.

Other people turn to 1 Corinthians 5:9 as "proof" that we should not engage in friendships with unbelievers: "I wrote you in my letter not to associate with immoral people." Seems pretty clear, doesn't it? Don't have relationships with unbelievers. But Paul also warned that some of them had misunderstood what he meant by immoral people. The apostle continues:

> I did not at all mean with the immoral people of this world, or with the covetous and swindlers, or with idolaters; for then you would have to go out of the world. But actually, I wrote to you not to associate with any so-called brother if he should be an immoral person, or covetous, or an idolater, or a reviler, or a drunkard, or a swindler—not even to eat with such a one. For what have I to do with judging outsiders? Do you not judge those who are within the church? But those who are outside, God judges. (1 Cor. 5:10-13)

Paul said that if you are going to "shun" anyone, shun immoral Christians, not unbelievers. Why? The apostle correctly reasons that it is impossible to live in this world without having some association with unbelievers. Furthermore, he explained, God never intended for us to judge unbelievers—that is his business. The people we *are* to judge are Christians who are living disobediently. Our purpose in refusing to associate with them is to convict them of the seriousness of their offense and restore them to a right relationship with God.

The Bible teaches that friendships with unbelievers are inevitable, permissible, and even desirable. But God's Word also gives some parameters to those relationships:

1. VIEW FRIENDSHIPS WITH UNBELIEVERS REDEMPTIVELY. While we may derive a certain amount of satisfaction from a friendship with an unbeliever, we are never to forget our responsibility to encourage that friend to become a Christian.

Of all the insults hurled against Jesus by the Pharisees, there is one he actually enjoyed—"a friend of sinners" (Matt. 11:19).

I think Jesus smiled every time he heard the Pharisees snarl that accusation. "A friend of sinners? Of course I am. Why do you think I gave up my position in heaven, if not to befriend and love those who are lost?" (See Luke 19:10.)

In the same way, God has not asked us to *isolate* ourselves from unbelievers. Nor does he want us to be *indifferent* toward unbelievers. Instead, we are to *influence* our non-Christian friends to become believers.

Think about one of your non-Christian friends or acquaintances. What positive actions could you take to encourage them to become a Christian? Do you pray for them every day? Have you invited them to church with you? Has your distinctive lifestyle as a Christian caused them to ask what makes you different from other people? As you think about that person, insert his name into Matthew 5:16: "Let your light shine before _____ in such a way that _____ may see your good works, and glorify your Father who is in heaven."

2. VIEW FRIENDSHIPS WITH UNBELIEVERS REALISTICALLY. By that, I mean not to expect your non-Christian friends to be your best friends.

Why? We have already seen that friendships are the result of things held in common with another person: experiences, likes and dislikes, location, interests, and a number of other factors. If our life revolves around our faith in Jesus Christ, then, obviously, that is something we cannot share in common with an unbeliever. That is why it is difficult, if not impossible, to share an intimate friendship with a non-Christian. What kind of intimacy could you ever hope to enjoy with a person with whom you could not share the most important aspect of your life?

This explains why God's Word prohibits marriage to a non-Christian, as we saw in chapter 6. It just doesn't work.

Problem #4: *"I'm married, but one of my closest friends is a member of the opposite sex. Is that wrong?"*

Ask your mate. He or she will be happy to tell you! Just kidding. This is a thorny issue that is seldom discussed. If it is addressed, most Christian books will make a blanket prohibition against such friendships. Better safe than sorry, they reason. But does such a restriction unnecessarily rob us of valuable friendships throughout our life?

For many people this is a nonissue. Remove the sexual aspect of the relationship, and many men cannot imagine establishing a friendship with a woman. "What in the world would I talk to another woman about? I have a hard enough time talking to my wife!" Likewise, many women might find it difficult to imagine any man, other than their husbands, with whom they could establish an intimate friendship—even if all sexual temptation were removed. It just seems . . . unnatural.

And yet there are some people who relate well to members of the opposite sex. Jesus Christ was one of those people. He was equally at ease with men and women. In fact, two of his most intimate friends were women—Mary and her sister, Martha. Jesus so valued his relationship with these two ladies that he chose to spend the last week of his earthly life with them.

"Oh, that's different," you say. "He was God—of course he could enjoy a platonic relationship with women."

But the Bible tells us that Jesus faced exactly the same temptations we face—including sexual ones. He was fully God, but he was also fully human. He had the same sex drives that other red-blooded Hebrew boys possessed. Yet Jesus was able to enjoy healthy, satisfying, and pure relationships with members of the opposite sex. Why should followers and imitators of Christ be prohibited from doing the same?

Before you consider initiating such relationships, however, let's look at two principles that should guide such relationships.

1. OUR SPOUSES SHOULD APPROVE OF THOSE FRIEND-SHIPS. Any friendship with a member of the opposite sex that is hidden from our spouse (or their spouse) has the potential for disrupting one or both marriages.

2. WE SHOULD REALIZE THAT ANY RELATIONSHIP WITH A MEMBER OF THE OPPOSITE SEX HAS THE POTENTIAL FOR EVIL. The best of people can do the worst of things.

Why is that? As we saw in chapter 2, the Bible teaches that we have all been infected with sin. The result of our sin nature is that we can take something beautiful—like friendship—and turn it into something ugly. And it can happen instantaneously. During a quiet lunch or dinner, a car ride, or a long walk, we can suddenly cross the line between friendship and emotional or physical intimacy that should be reserved for our spouse.

In addressing the subject of adultery, Solomon warned, "Can a man scoop fire into his lap without his clothes being burned? Can a man walk on hot coals without his feet being scorched?" (Prov. 6:27-28, NIV). Solomon was saying that some situations are too "hot" for anyone to handle—no matter how pure one's motives. A sexually oriented remark, a secret shared, a lingering embrace can quickly ignite into a raging fire. That is why friendships with members of the opposite sex are so dangerous. If you engage in one, stay away from "combustible" situations.

Problem #5: "I feel guilty about a friendship that has ended."

Bill and Jerry had been friends for years. Their children had grown up together, they worked in the same kind of business (though with different companies), and they had worshiped in the same church together for more than thirty years. But a controversy in the church had caused them to end up on opposite sides of the issue. For the last two years, Jerry had refused to speak to Bill, even though Bill had made many overtures of friendship to Jerry.

One day Bill was hauling a load of hay to his farm, about two hours south of his home. As he was driving down the lonely road, a car whisked by him in the passing lane. It was Jerry. Bill could not imagine what he was doing or where he was going. But he felt like this was divine providence that he would run into Jerry so far from home.

Bill sped up until his truck was even with Jerry's. He honked and waved, but Jerry would not respond. "Finally, I decided to follow Jerry to his destination. Maybe he would have a flat tire, and I would have the opportunity to assist him and demonstrate that I cared about him. I followed him for another hour, but nothing happened. I prayed for him and the restoration of our friendship the whole way."

Nothing is more painful, or more guilt inducing, than relationships that end—especially when we feel that we have contributed in some way to the dissolution of that friendship.

As we have said before, some friendships will naturally change due to uncontrollable circumstances. But there is a difference between friendships that change and those that end. Friendships that end usually do so over an offense, a misunderstanding, or an unmet expectation. How can we resolve those differences that can terminate a relationship? God's Word gives us two guidelines for resolving disputes:

1. FORGIVE THOSE FRIENDS WHO HURT YOU. Ephesians 4:32 gives us a formula for preserving relationships: "And be kind to one another, tender-hearted, forgiving each other, just as God in Christ also has forgiven you." The word *forgive* literally means "to release."

What a perfect picture of forgiveness! All of us are going to be offended by someone else—that is just a part of life. A friend may accidentally (or intentionally) say an unkind word, divulge a confidence, forget a birthday, or be unresponsive to a need. We cannot control what people do to us. But we *can* control our response to those offenses. We can choose to hold on to those offenses and become bitter. Or we can choose to let go of those offenses and experience emotional freedom. Paul says that we should release the offenses of others against us in the same way that God forgave our offenses against him.

2. RECONCILE WITH THOSE YOU HAVE HURT. A few years ago I received a letter from one of my best friends. He was a successful businessman and rarely wrote me a letter. Instead, we usually communicated by phone. So I was anxious to read his letter. When I ripped open the letter, I was surprised to find a detailed list of grievances this person had against me.

For the next several weeks I stewed in my anger. I decided that I would just write him off as a friend and move on. But then God brought to my mind the words of Matthew 5:23-24: "If therefore you are presenting your offering at the altar, and there remember that your brother has something against you, leave your offering there before the altar, and go your way; first be reconciled to your brother, and then come and present your offering."

Those words led me to swallow my pride and contact my friend. Though I did not think I had committed any offense deserving of such an epistle, he obviously felt differently. We both admitted some wrong on our part, and our friendship was salvaged.

That is a story with a happy ending. But Bill and Jerry's story did not have such an ending—at least not yet. Bill has made numerous attempts at reconciliation, but Jerry has chosen to reject those offers. The key to guilt-free friendships—especially those that end—is knowing that we have done everything we can to preserve and restore that relationship.

We have covered a lot of ground in these few pages. Yes,

friendships are difficult to establish, costly to preserve, and sometimes painful to endure. But guilt-free friendships are absolutely essential for our emotional health.

Do you have a handful of close friends like those described at the beginning of this chapter? If not, apply the principles of this chapter, and start developing some of those relationships *today*. Remember, it takes a long time to grow an old friend.

So far we have tackled the subjects of guilt-free life management and guilt-free relationships. Yet, even after you have learned how to say "enough" in those important areas, you still may feel there is one part of your life in which you need to do more, as we will see in the next chapter.

. . . . .

CHAPTER 10

Guilt-Free
Bible Study

I T is no secret that for the past fifteen years the denomination in which I serve (Southern Baptist) has been in a heated and divisive controversy over the Bible. Is the Bible totally free from historical and scientific error? If so, how should that belief affect the teaching in our denominational seminaries, colleges, and agencies?

This "battle for the Bible" is an important one, no doubt. If God's Word is filled with errors, why bother to study and apply it? Nevertheless, at a recent gathering of pastors, I was interested to hear one of the leaders of the inerrancy movement in our denomination confess that he had difficulty carving out enough time for personal Bible study. That struck me as interesting. Here is someone who is willing to place his career on the line to defend the truth of God's Word; yet like many of us, he has difficulty finding time to make the Bible a part of his own life.

His case is not unique. I am convinced that most Christians have a love/hate relationship with the Bible. Yes, they love

God's Word and are willing to defend it against the attacks of the "heathen." Yet they honestly hate the thought of actually studying the Bible themselves. They secretly harbor the same attitude toward Bible study as they do toward broccoli: "I know its good for me, but . . ."

A recent study by the Barna Research Group revealed that in an average week, only 10 percent of Americans read their Bible every day. And that figure is probably high. George Barna explains that many people who claimed to have read the Bible daily had not done so the week before this survey in 1991.[1]

A survey by George Gallup also reveals the ambivalent feelings many people have about the Word of God. Although 82 percent of Americans believe the Bible is the "inspired Word of God," half of them could not even name one of the four Gospels (Matthew, Mark, Luke, and John), and fewer than half knew who delivered the Sermon on the Mount.[2]

Whenever people consistently don't do what they know they should be doing, the result is guilt. As we have seen in previous chapters, that truth applies to saving money, managing time, losing weight, and raising children. Therefore, since most people know they should be studying the Bible, yet surveys reveal that they are not doing so, we can assume that many people feel guilty about their lack of Bible study. Maybe you are one of those people.

This chapter will give you some simple and practical steps to help you enjoy a lifetime of "guilt-free" Bible study. Along the way we will also knock down some of the unrealistic expectations about Bible study that keep people from enjoying a regular intake of God's Word.

First, let's identify some of the reasons Christians do not study the Bible.

BARRIERS TO BIBLE STUDY

1. Lack of a salvation experience

I will have to confess that I have used this possibility as a way to goad my congregation into the spiritual disciplines or into spiritual service: "Do you enjoy watching TV more than studying the Bible or praying? Would you rather be on the golf course than in church? If so, it may be because you are not a Christian."

The truth is that there are other reasons people may not pray, attend church, or study the Bible. In the next few pages we will outline some of those reasons. Nevertheless, a disinterest in God's Word may stem from a lack of a genuine salvation experience. A non-Christian may be fascinated with the Bible as a piece of great literature, but he will have little interest in studying and applying the truths of the Bible to his own life. Only Christians possess a genuine hunger for the Word of God.

The apostle Peter wrote, "Like newborn babes, long for the pure milk of the word, that by it you may grow in respect to salvation" (1 Pet. 2:2). When our two daughters were infants, they had little interest in football, art, the stock market, or the weather. They were fixated on one thing—*milk!* Morning, noon, night (and the middle of the night) they cried for milk. After a bottle, they were content—for a while. But every two or three hours an internal alarm went off, and they began screaming for another dairy "fix."

Their desire for milk was not an acquired taste. Amy and I did not have to teach them to crave milk. In fact, there was nothing we could do to diminish their insatiable appetite for it! Peter was saying that it should be the same way for anyone who has been born again into God's family. One evidence that we have God's Spirit residing in our lives is a constant desire to be fed from his Word.

I had the privilege of leading my future wife to faith in Christ when we were both freshmen in high school. Immediately after becoming a Christian, she had an extraordinary hunger for reading God's Word. She carried her New Testament to school and read it during breaks between classes. She would spend her evenings sitting on the deck of her home studying the Bible. Her parents were always chastising her for doing nothing else but reading "that Bible." In one of my most carnal thoughts of all time, I even regretted witnessing to her, because she had little time to spend with me anymore—she was too busy studying her Bible.

Maybe you had a similar experience when you became a Christian. That is the "norm" for true believers. On the other hand, if you have never experienced that kind of hunger for God's Word, it may be because you have never been born into God's family through faith in Jesus Christ.

2. *Viewing Bible study as a requirement rather than a privilege*

Recently I had an idea for an evangelistic program in our church. I told my administrative associate to contact the appropriate staff member and have him implement the program. My associate returned several days later and reported that the staff member was less than enthusiastic about the project. Why? The staff member said, "I feel like I am being forced to do this project. I would be a lot more excited if I had come up with the idea myself."

That is human nature. We all inwardly rebel against those things we feel are requirements. Exercise programs, diets, money management techniques, and programs to improve our marriages are many times doomed to failure because of the rebellious attitude we have toward those disciplines. We don't enjoy those things we feel are forced upon us. That attitude extends toward Bible study as well.

However, to quote the late President Nixon, "Let me make one thing perfectly clear." Bible study is a requirement for our spiritual growth. We saw that in 1 Peter 2:2: "Like newborn babes, long for the pure milk of the word, that *by it you may grow* in respect to salvation" (emphasis mine). Just as a baby will not grow apart from food, you will not grow in your faith apart from a regular feeding from God's Word.

But ask yourself the question Does a baby's desire for and intake of milk cause his parent to love him more? If the baby were sick or for some other reason had no desire for milk, would the parent love him any less? Of course not! If anything, a baby's lack of desire for food would cause the parent to become concerned—not angry. The parent would desire to do everything possible to make sure the baby received the sustenance he needed.

Bible study (or the lack of Bible study) does not result in God's loving us any more or any less than he already does. That is what grace is all about. The grace of God means that there is nothing we can do to make God love us any more or any less than he does already. The realization of that marvelous truth can give us a liberating attitude about Bible study. The study of God's Word is not some legalistic requirement to be satisfied, but a marvelous opportunity to know God more intimately.

3. Not knowing how to study the Bible

Everything I ever learned about Bible study—no, I didn't learn it in kindergarten—I learned in seminary from my friend and mentor Dr. Howard Hendricks. "Prof" Hendricks taught me a simple way to observe, interpret, and apply God's Word in a consistent way. I will never forget the new excitement I had about Bible study, now that I knew how to do it. In fact, I became so enthused about Bible study that I asked Dr. Hendricks to help me take his principles and teach them to laymen. The result was a weekend seminar for laymen called The Discovery Bible Seminar. For several years I traveled around the country teaching laymen the same principles Dr. Hendricks had taught me. (Since that time, Dr. Hendricks has published those Bible study principles in an excellent book entitled *Living by the Book*.)

I discovered in those two years of travel that there are many dedicated Christians who would love to study God's Word—but they don't know how. The Bible is a locked book for them, and they don't have the foggiest idea where to find the key. In *Living by the Book*, Dr. Hendricks quotes one intelligent woman's attitude about Bible study:

> Well, I went through a phase once where I decided I was really going to study the Bible. I'd heard someone at a seminar say that it's impossible to know God apart from knowing his Word. I knew I wanted to get closer to the Lord, so I made up my mind to really get into Scripture. I bought all these books about the Bible. I came home from work every night and spent about an hour or more reading and trying to understand it.
>
> But I realized that I didn't know Greek or Hebrew. And there are an awful lot of things that people were saying about different passages that made no sense to me. I mean, I'd read what somebody had to say about a text, and then I'd read the text, but I couldn't figure out how they'd come up with it. Finally, it just got so confusing, I quit.[3]

I believe a person can understand God's Word without knowing Greek and Hebrew and without a seminary degree. Later in this chapter I am going to share with you some simple methods to help you understand God's Word.

4. Failure to apply God's Word

Another reason some Christians become disinterested in studying the Bible is because they approach Bible study from a purely academic point of view. But God did not give us his Word to make us smarter sinners. God has interest in increasing not our level of knowledge, but our level of obedience.

There is truth to the statement "Light accepted bringeth more light; light rejected bringeth night." If we apply the light from God's Word that we understand, he will give us more light. But if we reject what we know to be true, he will darken our ability to understand his Word. The psalmist expressed the relationship between understanding God's Word and obeying God's Word when he wrote, "Teach me, O Lord, the way of Thy statutes, and I shall observe it to the end" (Ps. 119:33). Whenever we attempt to divorce Bible study from practical applications to our lives, the result will be confusion and eventually apathy.

5. Failure to understand the benefits of Bible study

Today I received in the mail a packet from our denomination's pension department. The purpose of the mailing was to encourage pastors to contribute more each month to their retirement program. In the packet was a large facsimile of a twenty-dollar bill that carried the words "What $20 will buy you: a movie for you and your wife, a pizza for your family, or a book for your library." Then on back of the bill were these words: "But look at what just a twenty-dollar per month increase in your retirement program will buy." There was a chart showing that such an increase for me would result in more than nineteen thousand dollars being added to my retirement account by the time I was ready to retire. Smart advertising. Those copywriters understood that admonishing me to quit wasting twenty bucks on pizza, movies, or books was not enough to make me save. They needed to show me the benefits of saving.

The reason most Christians neglect the study of God's Word, I believe, is because they are unaware of the benefits that come from studying and applying the Scriptures. Just look at some of the benefits of studying God's Word:

1. SPIRITUAL GROWTH. "Like newborn babes, long for the pure milk of the word, that by it you may grow in respect to salvation" (1 Pet. 2:2).

2. VICTORY OVER TEMPTATION. "How can a young man keep his way pure? By keeping it according to Thy word. . . . Thy word I have treasured in my heart, that I may not sin against Thee" (Psalm 119:9, 11).

3. SUCCESS IN SPIRITUAL SERVICE. "This book of the law shall not depart from your mouth, but you shall meditate on it day and night, so that you may be careful to do according to all that is written in it; for then you will make your way prosperous, and then you will have success" (Josh. 1:8).

4. FREEDOM FROM ANXIETY. "Finally, brethren, whatever is true, whatever is honorable, whatever is right, whatever is pure, whatever is lovely, whatever is of good repute, if there is any excellence and if anything worthy of praise, let your mind dwell on these things . . . and the God of peace shall be with you" (Phil. 4:8-9).

Spiritual growth, victory over temptation, success in spiritual service, and freedom from anxiety are just some of the benefits of studying and applying the Bible.

EXPERIENCING GUILT-FREE BIBLE STUDY

Now that we have identified some of the barriers to, as well as benefits of, Bible study, we are ready to answer the question

How can I experience guilt-free Bible study? Allow me to make several suggestions.

1. Throw away your "Read through the Bible in a Year" programs.

Before you label me a heretic, let me explain. For some of you, these programs may be beneficial. You enjoy a regimented program of three chapters from the Old Testament and one from the New Testament each day. Or maybe you are on a program of reading five psalms and one proverb each day. If that works for you, great!

But my experience with those programs is that people easily become more focused on "going through the Bible" than on allowing the Bible to go through them. For example, the alarm clock doesn't go off one morning (or some "mysterious" hand pushes the snooze button), and suddenly you find yourself in a mad rush to get out the door. There goes your morning Bible reading—but you will make it up that evening. Unfortunately, a late meeting at work delays your arrival home. When you do finally hit the front door, you have dinner to prepare or kids to bathe or some other responsibility. Finally, when bedtime rolls around, you can hardly keep your eyes open.

But you have committed—no, actually you made a "vow" to God—to read the entire Bible this year. Unfortunately, your Old Testament passage for tonight comes from 2 Kings—an endless record of king after king who "slept with his father" (an Old Testament expression for *died*). You race through those passages in an effort to enjoy some sleep yourself. You promise to do better tomorrow.

A steady diet of that kind of "Bible study" could make anyone learn to hate the Word of God! Who says you need to read the Bible through in a year? Since it took sixteen hundred years to write, what's the big hurry? Why not take two years to read the

Bible instead of one? Why not spend four months on the Psalms and three months on Proverbs?

The reason these artificial schedules seldom work is because all of us have different amounts of time to devote to Bible study. The retired person certainly has more time than the busy homemaker with three small children. Our individual days and schedules vary also. Some days we have more time to devote to Bible study than others.

There is a difference between having a plan and having a schedule of Bible study. For example, a plan would be to study the book of Romans. However, a schedule would dictate that the plan would be accomplished in a month.

I believe that Bible study schedules produce needless guilt, but Bible study plans produce spiritual growth.

2. Read the Bible in an understandable version.

The guilt some of us feel about not enjoying reading God's Word sometimes can be instantly alleviated by switching translations. I grew up in a strong evangelical church. But as a child and teenager, I never particularly enjoyed reading my King James Version of the Scriptures. Then one summer at our church's youth camp, God called me to be a pastor. When I returned home from camp that Friday afternoon, I had an immediate desire to read the Bible. Fortunately, my parents had just purchased the new paraphrase of the Scriptures—*The Living Bible*. That afternoon I locked myself in my room and started reading the book of Romans from *The Living Bible*. It was that summer that the Word of God came alive to me for the first time.

As I began my sophomore year at high school that fall, I carried my green *Living Bible* to school every day. I always stopped at a park near the school to spend half an hour reading God's Word. I memorized many of the psalms from that Bible and would quote them back to the Lord before I drifted off to sleep each evening. Certainly my call to the ministry was partly responsible for my new hunger for Bible study. But I also credit an easy-to-understand version of the Bible.

Gail Linam, a graduate of Southwestern Baptist Theological Seminary, concluded in her doctoral dissertation that the King James Version of the Bible frustrated children, sometimes to the point of tears. In an interview, she stated, "In reality, that beautiful language translated in 1611 represented a whole new language for the boys and girls, one that they didn't understand." As a part of her research, children were divided into three groups and asked to read a Bible story using the King James Version, the New International Version, or the New Century Version. Then they were filmed retelling the story to a research assistant. One girl from the King James Version group couldn't even begin to retell her story. "I don't know," she said, staring into the camera. "I didn't understand. This is too much stress for me."[4]

I don't think that little girl is alone. Many children, as well as adults, have been turned off to Bible study because of archaic translations. Many modern translations like the New International Version or the *New American Standard Bible* are much easier to understand and to read than the King James Version. Furthermore, many scholars believe these newer translations are actually more accurate in their translation of the Greek and Hebrew texts.

3. Read the Bible observantly.

Whether your Bible study schedule for the day allows you to read a verse, a paragraph, or an entire chapter, you will want to observe carefully everything in the text rather than racing through the passage.

I am a sucker for a good detective program. My favorite TV

detective of all time is Columbo. Columbo's ability to solve the crime by noticing small details others overlook has always fascinated me. When he enters the scene of the crime, you can almost hear his mind whirring as he analyzes each piece of evidence. Although everyone else has access to the same evidence as Columbo, he is always the one who solves the crime. Why? Because he knows what to look for.

When you come to a passage of Scripture, it is important to be a good observer. A skilled investigator of the Bible has to know what to look for. As the accompanying chart shows, there are two areas you should observe closely: content (What is being said?) and form (How is it being said?).

What to look for:

"WHAT IS SAID" (Content)	"HOW IT IS SAID" (Form)
Who? *Who are the people involved?*	Comparison-Contrast
What? *What is happening?*	Cause-Effect
When? *When did it take place?*	Repetition
Where? *Where is it taking place?*	Question-Answer
	Illustration
	Climax
SUMMARIZE	ANALYZE

1. CONTENT. Whenever someone asks you to describe a book you have read or a movie you have seen, you try to summarize it in terms of content. You will usually mention the subject (who), the action (what), the time period (when), and the location (where). You will usually be able to summarize the book or movie in a sentence or two. In your reading and

studying of the Bible, you should pause after each paragraph and try to summarize what you have read, using the same questions.

Here's a brief exercise. Read Mark 1:35, and then try to summarize the verse, using those four questions:

> "And in the early morning, while it was still dark, He arose and went out and departed to a lonely place, and was praying there."
>
> Who: _____
> What: _____
> When: _____
> Where: _____

The answers to those simple questions (who, what, when, and where) reveal some important principles about prayer. Jesus Christ, the Son of God (who); arose, went out and departed and prayed (what); in the early morning before it was light, on one of the busiest recorded days of his ministry (when); in a lonely place (where). If Jesus, the Son of God, thought prayer was that important, how much more vital is prayer for us? See how much you can discover by simply paying attention to content.

2. FORM. It is important to observe not only what is being said, but how it is being said. A good investigator of the Bible should be skilled in looking for many different forms of expression, some of which are noted on the accompanying chart. For example, Psalm 1 comes alive when you notice the sharp contrasts and picturesque comparisons that the psalmist paints. Other devices the biblical writers use to highlight their message include repetition, cause-effect relationships, questions and answers, illustrations, and climaxes. Remember, these are just *some* of the things you should look for in a passage of Scripture.

4. *Learn to interpret the Bible correctly.*

The correct interpretation of Scripture is vital to the proper application of Scripture. Unfortunately, many Christians feel they are unqualified to interpret the Bible—especially difficult passages—correctly. That's what preachers and seminary professors are for, they reason. But it is essential that all of us learn to interpret the Scripture accurately if we are going to apply it correctly.

Application depends strongly on interpretation. Suppose I left a note on the refrigerator for my wife saying that I had to take an unexpected business trip to Atlanta but needed her to pick me up at the airport at 10:00 on Wednesday. The only problem with my note is that I did not specify A.M. or P.M. My wife would be faced with the job of trying to interpret my message so that she could make the proper application. How could she determine if I meant A.M. or P.M.? She could show it to her friends and ask them what the note meant to them. But that would be meaningless. What is important is for her to determine what I meant, not what others think I meant. In the same way the student of Scripture must determine what the writer had in mind when he wrote a particular passage in order to be able to properly apply that passage of Scripture.

As an example, let's examine one difficult passage of Scripture that always leaves many Christians scratching their heads—James 2:24. "You see that a man is justified by works, and not by faith alone." What is James saying? Are we saved by faith and works? Obviously, the correct interpretation of this verse is vital to the application of this verse. What must we do to receive eternal life? Is faith enough? Or must faith in Christ be combined with good works?

To interpret this verse correctly, we must get into James's mind and discover what he meant when he wrote that "a man is justified by works, and not by faith alone." How can we discover what James was thinking nearly two thousand years ago when he penned these words? Four principles will help you discover the correct interpretation for any passage of Scripture.[5]

1. THE PRINCIPLE OF CONTEXT. Most difficult portions of Scripture can be easily understood by reading them in context—that is, considering the verses preceding and following the passage in question. For example, when I read the entire book of James, I understand that James is not trying to explain how a person is saved; instead, he is writing about the results that accompany a legitimate salvation experience. James assumes that his readers are already Christians (see James 1:18). His repeated use of the phrase *my brethren* indicates that James was not concerned about the eternal destiny of his readers— that was assumed. Instead, he was interested in his fellow Christians' living a life consistent with their profession of faith. Thus, looking at the general context of the passage helps us to understand the meaning of this passage.

2. THE PRINCIPLE OF COMPOSITION. Sometimes difficult portions of Scripture can be understood by looking up the meaning of key words in a good Bible dictionary. For example, in James 2:24, the key word to understand is the word *justified*. If you were to look that word up in a Bible dictionary, you would find that the word can mean (1) "to make righteous" or (2) "to show to be righteous." A careful examination of the passage reveals that James uses the word *justified* to mean "to show to be righteous." James is saying that our actions demonstrate our right relationship with God. On the other hand, the apostle Paul uses the term *justified* to mean "to make righteous." According to Paul, that aspect of justification comes by faith in Christ alone (see Rom. 3:28).

3. THE PRINCIPLE OF COMPARISON. The best commentary on the Bible is the Bible. Therefore, you should use other Scripture to help you interpret difficult passages. Since all the

Bible came from God, we can be sure that he will not contradict himself. For example, James 2:24 seems to teach that we are saved by works, not by faith. But other portions of the Bible clearly teach that we are justified (made right with God) by faith alone. For example, look at Ephesians 2:8-9: "For by grace you have been saved through faith; and that not of yourselves, it is the gift of God; not as a result of works, that no one should boast."

But Paul went on to say, "For we are His workmanship, created in Christ Jesus for good works, which God prepared beforehand, that we should walk in them" (Eph. 2:10). Thus, Paul and James are in agreement that while a person is made righteous by faith in Christ alone, that faith will express itself in concrete ways.

4. THE PRINCIPLE OF CONSULTATION. The final step in discovering the correct meaning of a passage is to consult other sources to see if your conclusions are in line with what other conservative scholars have found to be true. For example, I found this insightful comment on James 2:24 that explains the seeming contradiction between Paul's and James's views of justification:

> They [James and Paul] are not antagonists facing each other with crossed swords; they stand back to back, confronting different foes of the gospel. Paul is combating a Jewish legalism which insisted upon the need for works to be justified; James insists upon the need for works in the lives of those who have been justified by faith.[6]

Thus, by using the principles of context, composition, comparison, and consultation, I am able to discover what I call "the author's concept" (see chart). I now know what James meant when he wrote that a man is justified by works and not by faith alone. James simply means that true saving faith will always result in good works.

Principles of Interpretation

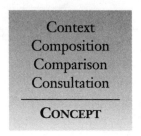

Context
Composition
Comparison
Consultation

CONCEPT

5. Make application the goal of your Bible study.

The goal of all Bible study should be a changed life! As I wrote earlier, one reason so many people are turned off by Bible study is because they see no relationship between the study of God's Word and their everyday life. How can a book written thousands of years ago apply to your work, family, relationships, and other life areas?

The key to the application of Scripture is finding "timeless principles" in the passage. A "timeless principle" is a truth about God, man, or Satan that supersedes time and culture. In other words, it is an eternal truth.

Why not try your hand at discovering the "timeless principles" from Ephesians 5? Use a modern translation, and see if you can list ten timeless truths from this passage.

Ten Timeless Truths from Ephesians

1. _____
2. _____
3. _____

4. _____
5. _____
6. _____
7. _____
8. _____
9. _____
10. _____

Discovering timeless truths is only the first step in applying Scripture. An application is a specific step of action you plan to take because of the timeless truth you uncovered. For example, one of the timeless principles from Ephesians 5 is that men are to demonstrate sacrificial love to their wives. That truth applies to every husband in every generation, right?

But I have not yet applied the Bible if I stop there. How does that truth impact my life? I must take that timeless principle and translate it into a specific step of action. What am I going to do differently in my life this week because of that truth? One thing I might do is agree to watch the kids Saturday morning so that Amy can have some time for herself. Or I might forego buying a new hard disk for my computer so that I can purchase a new dishwasher that she wants to make her work easier.

Here is another timeless principle from Ephesians 5. God wants us to refrain from any immoral behavior (v. 3). That's the principle, but how does that principle affect my relationships, my thought life, and my leisure time? Maybe one specific step of action would be to quit viewing a certain television program or stop subscribing to a particular magazine. Only when I have allowed God's timeless principles to impact my behavior have I really applied the Scriptures.

Here are some practical steps to begin a program of guilt-free Bible study:

1. If you don't already own one, purchase an easy-to-understand translation of the Bible. The *New American Standard Bible* and the New International Version are excellent translations.
2. Select a book of the Bible that you want to study. Ephesians, Philippians, or James would be a good place to begin.
3. Try to devote at least ten minutes a day to reading in the book of the Bible you have selected. It might work for you to do your Bible study at the same time every day—it might not. Consistency is a worthy goal—but don't berate yourself if you have to miss a day or two.
4. As you read, observe carefully the content and form of what you are reading. It is better to read one paragraph and comprehend what you are reading than to scan large portions of Scripture and retain nothing! Don't be afraid to mark in your Bible your observations. (For more information on what to observe and mark in your Bible study, see the already mentioned *Living by the Book* by Howard and William Hendricks, published by Moody Press).
5. When you have difficulty understanding what you are reading, use the principles of interpretation we have discussed.
6. Never conclude your Bible study without developing at least one specific step of action you will take that day to apply what you have studied.

Here's a money-back guarantee! If you engage in this type of Bible study plan for a month, you will find that ten minutes of Bible study growing to twenty minutes, thirty minutes, and even an hour. And your motivation will no longer be guilt, but a genuine hunger for the truth of God's Word, which is "sweeter also than honey and the drippings of the honeycomb" (Ps. 19:10). Sure sounds better than a plateful of broccoli, doesn't it?

Another area of our spiritual lives that is often thought of as a ritual, rather than a privilege, is the subject of the next chapter.

CHAPTER 11

. . . . .

Guilt-Free
Praying

SAMUEL Logan Brengle was a "prayer warrior." As an evangelist for the Salvation Army, Brengle bathed his ministry in prayer. One biographer notes, "At prayer he was a study in communion. It was his habit, except for those periods when he was too ill, to get out of bed between four and five o'clock in the morning and devote at least a full hour before breakfast to communion with his Lord."[1] Examine the lives of great men and women of God through the centuries—Hudson Taylor, Susanna Wesley, George Whitefield—and you will find similar patterns of prayer.

Here's my problem. As challenged as I am by these accounts of early and extended prayer times, I can't duplicate them. I want to, but I can't. Although I might be able to pull myself out of bed at four in the morning to pray, I would not be worth killing the rest of the day. Furthermore, if I were to try to pray before breakfast, I would find myself focusing on images of an Egg McMuffin rather than God the Father.

No, I'm not a lazy person. I continue to accomplish many

things in my ministry. But I know my limits. And early, extended prayer in the morning is not for me.

I don't think I am alone. I believe you may be one of those Christians who would sincerely like to pray more. The thought of hours of uninterrupted intercession is actually appealing to you. Yet the responsibilities of work, family, ministry, and even recreational pursuits make it difficult to carve out large blocks of time for prayer. The result is that you may have given up prayer altogether (except for the occasional back-up-against-the-wall prayers: "Lord, get me out of this mess.").

I believe there is a better way. In this chapter we will try to explode some myths about prayer that hinder many believers from enjoying the benefits of regular, intimate encounters with God. In exposing those unrealistic expectations, we will also become aware of what the Bible *does* say about prayer. Second, I will suggest some practical steps that will help you begin a reasonable program of prayer in spite of a hectic and changing schedule.

PHARISEES ARE ALIVE AND WELL . . . AND ARE PRAYING IN YOUR CHURCH

Carefully examine the teachings of Jesus Christ, and you will discover an interesting fact. Jesus did not condemn murderers, drunkards, or adulterers. Instead, he simply forgave them. But Jesus did regularly condemn one group of people—religious people! Jesus' harshest words were directed against the Pharisees, that sect of Judaism that placed their own traditions as equal to the authority of God's Word. Specifically, the Pharisees added their own traditions, rituals, and prejudices to the simple requirements of the Word of God. Look at what Jesus said about these Pharisees:

And they tie up heavy loads, and lay them on men's shoulders; but they themselves are unwilling to move them with so much as a finger. . . . But woe to you, scribes and Pharisees, hypocrites, because you shut off the kingdom of heaven from men; for you do not enter in yourselves, nor do you allow those who are entering to go in. (Matt. 23:4, 13)

The result of the Pharisees' teaching was that Judaism had become an unbearable load of rules and regulations that no one was capable of keeping. Thus, the majority of people simply gave up trying to live a righteous life.

The same thing has happened in the church today. We have our own incarnation of Pharisees who are not content with the simple teachings of the New Testament. Instead, they want to add to the requirements for Christian living found in Scripture. You regularly hear their radio programs, read their books, and attend their seminars. Some go back to the Old Testament and pull out laws about diets, or clothing, or money management and place Christians under an unbearable load of guilt. Others simply take their own practices and prejudices about parenting, marriage, music, or dress and canonize them as "principles."

Unfortunately, the result has been that many people—unable to meet all of these unrealistic and unnecessary expectations—have given up trying to adhere to *any* biblical principles in their lives. The Pharisees have once again succeeded in "shutting off the kingdom of heaven from men."

In this chapter we want to untangle the man-made rules and regulations about prayer from the simple teaching of God's Word so that the doors of heaven are once again open to the average Christian. First, we must identify these barriers to guilt-free praying.

FIVE MYTHS THAT MAY KEEP YOU FROM EVER PRAYING

Myth #1: "I must spend hours in prayer each day for God to hear me."

Somehow, people have confused the length of a prayer with the earnestness of a prayer. While God certainly honors earnest prayer, he does not particularly enjoy lengthy prayers. In fact, Jesus leveled strong criticism against those who tried to impress God with a lot of words: "And when you are praying, do not use meaningless repetition, as the Gentiles do, for they suppose that they will be heard for their *many words*" (Matt. 6:7, emphasis mine).

In Jesus' day the Gentiles confused the quantity of words with the quality of prayer. The longer the prayers, the better. The Pharisees also believed that they could gain God's attention by the repetition of certain words and phrases. But Jesus said the opposite: God does not delight in "meaningless repetition" and "many words."

Please note that Jesus was not saying it is wrong to ask God for something more than once. You will remember that Jesus himself asked God three different times to keep him from the cross (see Matt. 26:39-44). The apostle Paul begged God to remove his thorn in the flesh on three separate occasions (see 2 Cor. 12:7-8). Yet neither Christ's nor Paul's repeated prayers caused God to act as they desired.

Some of the most effective prayers in the Bible were extremely brief. Remember Jesus' story about the tax gatherer and the Pharisee who went to the temple to pray? Which prayer did God hear? It was the tax gatherer's short but sincere prayer: "God, be merciful to me, the sinner!" (Luke 18:13).

Or consider Elijah's prayer on Mount Carmel. In his attempt to persuade the Israelites to renounce Baal and follow after the Lord, Elijah proposed a contest with the prophets of Baal. Whichever god would answer from heaven with fire and burn the sacrifice on the altar would be recognized as the true God.

First Kings 18:28-29 records the futile efforts of the Baal worshipers to move the hand of their god:

> So they cried with a loud voice and cut themselves according to their custom with swords and lances until the blood gushed out on them. And it came about when midday was past, that they raved until the time of the offering of the evening sacrifice; but there was no voice, no one answered, and no one paid attention.

Contrast their three hours of repeated prayer with the simple prayer of Elijah recorded in verses 36-37:

> O Lord, the God of Abraham, Isaac and Israel, today let it be known that Thou art God in Israel, and that I am Thy servant, and that I have done all these things at Thy word. Answer me, O Lord, answer me, that this people may know that Thou, O Lord, art God, and that Thou hast turned their heart back again.

I timed that prayer—it takes less than a minute to say. In the English text it contains only sixty-four words. Yet look at the result of that brief prayer. "Then the fire of the Lord fell, and consumed the burnt offering and the wood and the stones and the dust, and licked up the water that was in the trench" (1 Kings 18:38).

This story should forever bury the belief that you must spend hours praying to have an effective prayer life.

Myth #2: *"I should use a formula in my praying."*

You have probably heard of the prayer acrostic built on the word ACTS. Supposedly, this provides a guide to praying: *Adoration* (praising God for who he is—supposedly this is the part of our prayers that God "enjoys" the most); *Confession* (we must name our sins, or God can't hear anything else we say—unless we have some more adoration to voice); *Thanksgiving* (expressing gratitude for all that God has done); and *Supplication* (asking God for something—this should be last because supposedly this is the least important part of our prayer). This acrostic may be helpful in reminding us of different types of prayers. Certainly Jesus Christ himself gave us a model of prayer (see Matthew 6:9-13). However, the danger of such a "formula" is that it takes the joy and spontaneity out of prayer.

For example, suppose you attend a seminar on communication in marriage. During the seminar, the speaker says that you should learn to communicate with your spouse about a variety of topics—finances, parenting responsibilities, sexual needs, goals in life, and so on. The next Friday night, you and your mate are out at dinner. You are freely sharing with your mate about some of your frustrations at work when he says, "I would love to hear more about that, but time is running out, and we have not yet covered our children, our bills, or our sex life in this conversation." Talk about destroying intimacy! The truth is there are some times when you want to talk only about one topic with your spouse. There are other times when you run through a variety of subjects. Many times you have no agenda at all. Hopefully, your spouse listens to you out of genuine love for you, not because of your adherence to some communication method you have learned. We need to translate that truth to our prayer life.

Too many Christians believe that effective praying is the result of using magical theological words that somehow unlock the power of God. My favorite episode of the old TV show *All in the Family* was the one in which Archie Bunker was asked to give the eulogy (which he called the "urology") and prayer at a friend's funeral. Archie, terrified at the prospect of praying in public, asked his son-in-law to write the prayer for him. "Make sure and throw some 'Jesuses' in there," Archie admonished, certain that would cause God to listen.

There is no "formula" for effective praying. We need to come back to the simple understanding that prayer is not a theological formula, but an intimate conversation with someone who loves us and is vitally interested in every part of our lives. John Bunyan wrote, "Prayer is a sincere, sensible, affectionate pouring out of the heart or soul to God, through Christ."[2]

Myth #3: "I must pray in the morning."

I'm convinced that most people who write books about the spiritual disciplines in life must be morning people. That's all right until they start confusing their spirituality with their metabolism! We are all different. Some are more alert in the morning, others in the afternoon, still others late at night. My brother-in-law is a pastor. He sleeps until about nine o'clock every morning. A sluggard you say? Not really. He also stays up until two o'clock in the morning studying for his sermons—it works for him.

Let's quit using Psalm 5:3 and Mark 1:35 as a rule for when to pray. "In the morning, O Lord, you hear my voice; in the morning I lay my requests before you and wait in expectation" (Ps. 5:3, NIV). Mark 1:35 tells us that "in the early morning, while it was still dark, [Jesus] arose and went out and departed to a lonely place, and was praying there." Jesus was a morning person (though I doubt you often found him up at 2:00 A.M.). I'm sure this is one way I will never be like Jesus.

However, the Bible says we are to pray at all times—not just in the morning. In his booklet *The Disciple's Prayer*, John Mac-Arthur notes some of the different times that people in the Bible prayed:[3]

> early morning (Mark 1:35)
> morning (1 Chron. 23:30)
> midnight (Acts 16:25)
> daily (Ps. 86:3)
> day and night (Luke 2:37; 18:7)
> three times a day (Dan. 6:10)
> today (Ps. 95:6, 8)
> before meals (Matt. 14:19)
> after meals (Deut. 8:10)
> ninth hour (Acts 3:1)
> evening (1 Kings 18:36)
> bedtime (Ps. 4:4)
> in youth (Jer. 3:4)
> in trouble (2 Kings 19:3-4)
> often (Luke 5:33)
> always (Luke 18:7)

Myth #4: "God will not answer my prayers if there is any unconfessed sin in my life."

Perhaps you have heard people use the verse "If I regard wickedness in my heart, the Lord will not hear" (Ps. 66:18) to support this myth. The argument goes that since God is a holy God, he cannot have fellowship with sin. Therefore, unconfessed sin in our lives is like a barrier that hinders our prayers from ascending to heaven.

However, there is one small problem with this logic. The Bible says that Christ died for all our sins so that we might receive forgiveness. Consider these verses:

By this will we have been sanctified through the offering of the body of Jesus Christ once for all. . . . But He, having offered one sacrifice for sins for all time, sat down at the right hand of God. (Heb. 10:10, 12)

And not through the blood of goats and calves, but through His own blood, He entered the holy place once for all, having obtained eternal redemption. (Heb. 9:12)

For by one offering He has perfected for all time those who are sanctified. (Heb. 10:14)

Now, here's an important question. When Christ died on the cross, *which* sins did he die for? Obviously, he died for *all* of our sins. Remember, at the time of Christ's death all of our sins were still future. These verses clearly teach that Christ's death was sufficient to pay the penalty for and cleanse us from all of our sins. Now, if that is true, how can any of our sins break our fellowship with God and hinder our prayers if Christ has already dealt with them?

I believe that the sins we commit as Christians do not change God's attitude about us, but they change our attitude about God. I think about the couple that was on the way to dinner to celebrate their twenty-fifth wedding anniversary. As the husband was driving, the wife began to complain: "Honey, remember how it was when we were dating and then first married? We used to sit so close together in the car, and now look at us. You're on that side, and I'm way over here." The husband replied, "Dear, I haven't moved."

So it is in our relationship with God. He never moves. But sin causes us to move away from God. Confessing our sins as Christians is not necessary to gain God's forgiveness—that was secured at the cross of Christ. However, acknowledging our failures to God is important for us to move back into a right frame of mind about God.

Don't fall into the trap of thinking everything in your life must be perfect before you pray. First of all, you will never be sinless. And second, prayer itself is many times the pathway that leads you back into a right relationship with God.

Myth #5: "I should not ask God for 'selfish' requests."

Unfortunately, we have allowed some of the superspiritual saints to convince us that every time we ask God for something personal—like good health, a raise, a promotion, a new car, success, a mate, or any other number of requests—he grimaces and thinks, *You selfish, immature Christian. Why aren't you more interested in the salvation of the lost or proclaiming my glory throughout the world? You need to grow up!*

But when I look at the words of Jesus, I find that is not God's attitude at all. Remember his words about prayer in the Sermon on the Mount?

> Ask, and it shall be given to you; seek, and you shall find; knock, and it shall be opened to you. For everyone who asks receives, and he who seeks finds, and to him who knocks it shall be opened. Or what man is there among you, when his son shall ask him for a loaf, will give him a stone? Or if he shall ask for a fish, he will not give him a snake, will he? If you then, being evil, know how to give good gifts to your children, how much more shall your Father who is in heaven give what is good to those who ask Him! (Matt. 7:7-11)

As I write these words, it is a few days before Christmas. My five-year-old daughter has made very clear what she would like to discover with her name on it under the tree. She has circled it in red in the toy catalog! My two-year-old can't verbalize what she wants, but every time the ad comes on television for a talking Barney, her eyes light up. Yes, I know what my kids want for Christmas. And nothing will give me greater pleasure than watching their expressions as they unwrap their desired gifts along with a few surprises I've planned.

Jesus is using the same analogy. If we as earthly parents delight in giving our children what they want, how much more does our heavenly Father desire to give good gifts "to those who ask him"! Why should we think it strange that God would want to give us what we ask? Obviously, there are gifts my children might ask for that I might think are harmful or just premature for them to receive. I hope that my children's conversations with me are not limited to just their wish list. Nevertheless, I am not insulted when they ask me for a gift. I am thrilled to be able to answer their requests.

I just finished looking over my prayer requests list for the last four years. I would say that 90 percent of the requests fall under the category of "selfish"—everything from a success in an investment deal to a good report from the doctor. And guess what? God has answered most every one of those requests. Why? He delights in giving good gifts to his children and having us express our thanks to him. Just like my girls will do in a few days.

SEVEN HABITS OF A HIGHLY EFFECTIVE PRAYER LIFE

Now that we have exposed some of the myths about a successful prayer life, let's look at some positive suggestions for enjoying regular and intimate conversations with God. I realize that I have used many personal examples in the following section—perhaps too many. But mine is the only prayer life I know about.

Maybe some of my discoveries about what works and doesn't work will help you.

1. Begin and end each day in prayer.

Here is my ideal schedule each morning. I like to get up at 6:00 A.M., exercise, shower, drink a cup of coffee, and eat a bowl of bran flakes, get to the office by 7:30 A.M. and have my "quiet time," which consists of reading two chapters of the Bible, going through my prayer list, and making an entry in my spiritual journal. Unfortunately, I do well to keep that schedule 50 percent of the time. The other times, a crisis at church, needing to drop one of my kids off at school, an alarm that doesn't go off, a late night before, or just a case of not wanting to get up keeps me from my ideal schedule. But what I have learned is that such "setbacks" need not rob me of communicating with God.

On these days I detour from my ideal schedule, I can still begin each day with a simple prayer that sets the tone for the rest of my day. "Dear God, thank you for the gift of life. You know all that I have to do today. Help me to accomplish your goals for my life and be sensitive to your leading in every situation. Protect my family today in all that they do. In Christ's name, amen." In the same way, the last thing I do before I drift off to sleep each night is to thank God for what he has done in my life that day, confess my failures, ask his protection for our family during the night and tell him about my concerns. I remember the words of the late Mary Crowley, who said, "The last thing I do before I go to sleep is turn over all my problems to God. I figure he's going to be up all night anyway."

This kind of prayer life is not enough to sustain and mature one's relationship with God over the long haul. But such simple times of prayer keep us in touch with our heavenly Father when our schedules get the best of us. Those brief times of prayer will also increase our spiritual thirst for longer periods of time alone with God.

2. *Imagine God as a partner in every activity throughout the day.*

The apostle Paul commanded us to "pray without ceasing" (1 Thess. 5:17). What does that mean? Certainly Paul is not suggesting that we walk around in a hypnotic trance, mumbling to ourselves. The phrase *without ceasing* means to pray with the frequency of a hacking cough. You know *(hack, hack)* what Paul is *(hack, hack, hack)* talking about *(hack)* when he writes about a persistent, uncontrollable cough. Try to suppress it, and you can for a while. But soon you feel the tickle in your throat, and you can't control yourself.

Paul was saying that our prayers should emerge from our spirit with that kind of frequency. No matter what we are doing, we should be consistently talking with God, expressing our dependence upon him. In his *Testament of Devotion*, Thomas Kelly writes:

> There is a way of ordering our mental life on more than one level at once. On one level we can be thinking, discussing, seeing, calculating, meeting the demands of external affairs. But deep within, behind the scenes, at a profounder level, we may also be in prayer and adoration, song and worship, and a gentle receptiveness to divine breathings.[4]

To illustrate specific ways you might implement this practice:

When you are driving in the car: "Lord, keep me safe from any accidents."

When you are in a meeting: "Lord, help me to say what

you want me to say. What would be the right decision in this matter?"

When you are meeting a new person: "Lord, help me to discern the needs of this person. Give me a chance to say a word about you."

When you have received some exciting news: "Lord, thank you for this. I realize it is from you. Thank you for being so good to me."

When you receive distressing news: "Lord, I don't understand. Give me your strength to get through this."

It is both a simple and a profound concept. We don't limit our prayer life to extended and uninterrupted periods. Such thinking will rob us of the joy of conversing with God regularly. Instead, to pray without ceasing means to talk to God continually—about everything. Some might argue that this idea reduces the glory of God to the mundane activities of life. No, just the opposite! Regular communication with our Creator glorifies God as it reminds us of our absolute dependence upon him for everything.

3. Keep a record of your prayer requests and God's answers.

In my desk drawer I keep a legal pad that is divided down the middle with a black line. At the top of the left-hand column I have placed the words *My Requests*. The top of the right-hand column is labeled *God's Answers*. I place all of my requests under the left-hand column and date them. Obviously, some of those requests are ongoing: my health, my family's safety, the spiritual unity of our church, and so on. However, other requests are very specific. When they are answered either positively or negatively, I record that answer under the heading *God's Answers* and date it. Then I draw a single line through that request and answer. As one page fills up, I go to a second page until the tablet is completely filled. Then I take any of the unanswered or ongoing requests and transfer them to a new tablet.

This habit has done more to enhance my prayer life than any other. Let me mention benefits of keeping this kind of record.

First, such a list gives you something to pray about every day. We can quickly become distracted in our prayer time without a definite list of prayer concerns.

Second, the answered requests give you many things for which to thank God. Our heavenly Father does delight in our expressions of gratitude—just as those of us who are parents enjoy hearing our children say thank you.

And finally, a prayer list can remind you of God's faithfulness in the past and give you courage for the future.

The last several days I have been sick with the flu. While at home I did not feel like reading anything heavy, and I quickly tired of the daytime television fare. So I pulled out some of my old prayer journals and spent several hours reading though my requests and God's answers over the last several years. I was impressed by the faithfulness of God shown by his answers to my needs. But I also experienced genuine relief from some of my current concerns as I reflected on God's previous interventions in my life.

If you have never kept a prayer record, let me encourage you to begin immediately. It will focus your prayer time and will provide needed reminders of God's goodness in your life. And if you are ever sick, a prayer journal sure beats *Donahue*.

4. When others ask you to pray for them, do so immediately.

How many times has someone shared a problem with you, and as the conversation winds down you say, "I will be praying for you." And that is the last time you ever think about the request. That unkept promise robs the other person of the power of your prayer. But it can also be a source of guilt for you, as well.

On the other hand, if you keep all the prayer promises you make, you will find yourself with innumerable requests—some important, others not so important—that can quickly fill up your prayer time.

A better way to handle these requests is to offer to pray with the other person on the spot. "Would you mind if I just prayed for you right now?" No, this is not just a time-saving "technique." If done sincerely, this kind of praying can be a tremendous encouragement to the other person as well as relieve you of the guilt of unkept promises. Most important, this habit allows you to regularly intercede for someone else.

5. Make God the audience of your prayers.

Praying verbally for another person's request can be a great encouragement to that person. However, that is not the major purpose of prayer. I am continually amazed at the number of Christians who do not understand that the primary purpose of prayer is conversing with God, not building intimacy or offering encouragement to other believers.

For example, how many times have you read or heard that you should pray regularly with your spouse? But a survey by *Leadership* magazine revealed that only 20 percent of Christian leaders pray with their spouses daily.[5] Therefore, since Christians are being told they should pray with their spouse, and yet most Christians don't pray with their mate, there are many Christians who must feel guilty about their failure to meet this standard.

However, press the marriage "experts" about *why* we should pray with our spouse, and the answer is "to build intimacy with them." Now, I am all for intimacy—but that is not the purpose of prayer. Prayer is to build intimacy with *God*, not other people. Furthermore, as I search the Bible I cannot find one single admonition for Christians to pray with their spouses.

(The one verse that is sometimes cited is 1 Corinthians 7:5: "Stop depriving one another [of sexual intimacy], except by agreement for a time that you may devote yourselves to prayer, and come together again lest Satan tempt you because of your lack of self-control." But there is no reason to think that the prayer described here is joint prayer with one's spouse. Most probably Paul is referring to individual prayer.)

Other people emphasize the importance of group prayer. They say that group praying encourages other believers. One of the fine leaders of our church came to me recently and said, "Pastor, we would like to hear you pray more often. It would be an encouragement to our people." I appreciated the spirit in which he came, but he, too, missed the point of prayer. Prayer is not for the spiritual edification of the saints.

Whenever I think about group prayer, I think about a meeting my parents once attended. An older man, trying to impress the rest of the crowd with his spirituality, started his prayer by reviewing the attributes of God. Then he started praying for all the continents. Finally, it was time for the summation. "And, Lord, when the day comes that we cross the . . ." He could not think of the word *Jordan*. So he backed up and started again. "And, Lord, when the day comes that we cross the . . . *equator* . . ." That broke the group up and ended the prayer meeting.

I can sympathize with that man. When I do have to pray publicly, my attention is centered on what I'm saying, how I sound, the right choice of words, not repeating myself, making sure I include everything in my prayer I should, and so on. In times of group prayer, I am more concerned with planning what I am going to say than concentrating on the prayers of others. When I am finished, I feel like I have talked to everyone except God.

I do not think I am the only one with this problem. Most people cannot have two audiences for their prayers. They are either focusing on God or other people as their audience. I believe that is why Jesus said:

> And when you pray, you are not to be as the hypocrites; for they love to stand and pray in the synagogues and on the street corners, in order to be seen by men. Truly I say to you, they have their reward in full. But you, when you pray, go into your inner room, and when you have shut your door, pray to your Father who is in secret, and your Father who sees in secret will repay you. (Matt. 6:5-6)

Please don't misunderstand. I am not advocating that all churches cancel their prayer meetings and every believer retreat to his closet to pray. Read the book of Acts, and you will see that much of the success of the early church was because of corporate prayer. But I am not convinced that corporate prayer must always be verbalized. If you can pray out loud with your spouse or with other people and still maintain your focus on God, more power to you! But if you are like me, refuse to allow other well-meaning, but misdirected, believers pile on a load of unnecessary guilt about praying verbally with others. God, not other people, needs to be the audience for your prayers.

6. *Trust in the* sovereignty *of God in answering your prayers.*

A "Peanuts" cartoon strip featured Linus writing a letter to Santa Claus: "Dear Santa, Please don't bother to come to my house this year. I realize that there are many other more deserving kids. Really, it does not bother me if you don't stop by my house at all. Go to someone more needy." Lucy walks by and happens to read the letter. In exasperation she says, "What kind of letter is that?" Linus responds, "I'm hoping he'll find my attitude particularly refreshing."

Many of us are like Linus in our attitude about prayer. We think that if we have the right attitude, ask the right things, ask often enough, and jump through all the necessary spiritual "hoops," then maybe God will answer our requests. Conversely, when God does not answer our request, we assume responsibility for the negative reply. "If only I had prayed longer, given more sacrificially to the church, witnessed more, or removed this sin from my life, God would have answered my requests."

Such reasoning produces all kinds of unnecessary guilt. Answers to prayer are the result of God's sovereign plan, not our perfection (or imperfection). I mentioned earlier about the day I spent reviewing my prayer lists from the past few years. I saw that about four years ago I had prayed for about six months for several specific requests—things relating to my career, my finances, and my family. When there was no reply, I finally quit, reasoning that these things must not be in God's plan for my life.

Yet, within the last eighteen months, all of those requests have been answered. Why has God answered those requests now and not four years earlier? I am convinced that the reason has nothing to do with me, but with God's sovereign plan. He brought those changes in my life when it was his time.

Earlier we looked at Jesus' and Paul's repeated requests to remove the experience of the Cross and Paul's thorn in the flesh. In both cases God said no. But in neither case was the negative reply due to any lack of spirituality on the part of Jesus or Paul. Instead, God's negative reply was in keeping with his sovereign plan. Someone has said, "The only requests that are beyond the realm of prayer are those outside the will of God." Those who are effective prayers learn to trust in God's sovereignty for answered prayers and refuse to feel guilty when God says no or wait.

7. Be persistent in your prayers.
My friend Max Anders writes, "Most of us don't pray as much

as we feel we should, not because we are unwilling, but because we are uncertain how to pray and don't understand why our prayers aren't answered more consistently. It is frustrating to keep doing something that you are not sure is working."⁶ Jesus Christ encouraged us to be persistent in our prayers, even when the answers seem to be delayed. To illustrate that principle, Jesus told a parable about a widow who persistently pesters an unrighteous judge for justice. Finally, the judge gives in and answers her request.

Some could misinterpret the story to mean that God is like an unrighteous judge who must be coerced into answering our prayers. But Jesus makes it clear that his parable is one of contrast, not comparison:

> Now shall not God bring about justice for His elect, who cry to Him day and night, and will He delay long over them? I tell you that He will bring about justice for them speedily. (Luke 18:7-8)

In other words, if repeated requests can move an unrighteous judge to act on behalf of a widow for whom he has no special affection, how much more can our requests move a loving God to act on behalf of us who are his children? The word translated "speedily" does not mean immediately. The original word *(en-tachei)* means "with rapidity." In other words, whenever the answer begins to unfold, it will do so quickly and without interruption. Imagine a long line of dominoes, one right behind the other. As soon as you tip that first domino over, you set off a chain reaction that is hard to stop. Jesus is saying that if we are persistent in our praying (and, obviously, are praying according to God's sovereign plan), we can be certain that God will answer our prayers in his time.

Yes, I realize there is a contradiction here. On one hand, Jesus said we should not be like unbelievers who think God is impressed by "meaningless repetition" and "many words." Yet Jesus also affirms that God rewards earnestness and consistency in praying. Perhaps we can revert back to the child-parent analogy to understand what the Lord is communicating. When my child asks me for something once, I am not sure if it is a sincere desire or a capricious request—maybe my child is not even sure. But when my daughter asks me for something repeatedly, I know it is important to her. And when I do grant her request, she is grateful.

Obviously, God knows our heart—what is important to us and what is not. But maybe the reason God rewards repeated requests is that they make the answers all the more special to us when they come.

In this chapter I have emphasized that prayer is simple communication with our heavenly Father. It is talking to God honestly about our hopes, our fears, our desires, our failures. I have emphasized that we should bring our requests to God. He is a perfect father who delights in giving his children good gifts.

But prayer is more than these things. Ultimately, prayer is coming into the presence of almighty God. Whether you have an hour or just ten minutes, I hope this chapter will free you of unnecessary guilt about your prayer life and motivate you to spend time each day in the presence of God. I can promise that you will become a different person.

Now that you are reading your Bible and praying more, you may be feeling pretty good about yourself—until someone reminds you that there is something *else* you need to do to please God.

. . . . .

CHAPTER 12

Guilt-Free Ministry

I would rather have my fingers slammed shut in the door than go to work in children's worship this morning!"

We laughed, but I knew this deacon was serious. Twenty-five years ago, the church I serve began a bus ministry that reached about five hundred children each week. But over the years, the effectiveness of the ministry has diminished. To many, the bus ministry had become just a free baby-sitting service for disinterested parents. A number of the deacons had said to me privately, "We need to reevaluate the viability of this ministry or make some changes that will allow us to minister more effectively."

Fine, I thought. So I asked our minister of education to form a task force to look at our bus ministry. Guess what? Some who were complaining the loudest refused to serve on the committee. Why? They did not want to be responsible for possibly ending a ministry to children. They could not handle the guilt.

(I can't be too hard on those deacons. Instead of making the decision myself, I wanted *them* to handle it!)

What role does guilt play in ministry? Does it sometimes goad people into ministries for which they are not really gifted? Does guilt make it hard for people to say no when someone asks them to fill a position in the church?

Do you ever allow the ministry successes of others to rob you of joy in the ministry God has given you? Do you feel like a failure when someone rejects your invitation to become a Christian? Do you allow guilt to keep you in ministry positions for which you are no longer suited?

If your response is yes to any of the above questions, then you are a candidate for experiencing guilt-free ministry.

No Way Out

We should clarify what is meant by "guilt-free ministry" by stating two biblical presuppositions about ministry:

1. Every Christian is to be involved in ministry.

In Ephesians 4:11-12, Paul gave us the pattern for ministry in the local church:

> And He gave some as apostles, and some as prophets, and some as evangelists, and some as pastors and teachers, for the equipping of the saints for the work of service, to the building up of the body of Christ.

What is the role of the pastor and other staff members in the church? They are to "equip the saints for the work of service." That word translated "equip" (*kartamismon* in Greek) originally referred to the loading of a ship with supplies before embarking on a long journey. Thus, Paul was saying that the primary role of the pastor and staff is to give members the supplies they need to perform "the work of service" or ministry. As we will see later, there is a variety of services different members might perform in the body of Christ: for example, some serve as teachers, others serve as administrators, and others perform service ministries. But every Christian is to perform some service that contributes to the "building up of the body of Christ."

The late Bud Wilkinson served as the chairman of the President's Council for Physical Fitness during the Johnson administration. Someone once asked Wilkinson what role professional football had played in America's physical fitness. "Absolutely none. In football you have twenty-two players on the field desperately in need of rest being cheered on by fifty thousand spectators in the stands desperately in need of exercise!" Unfortunately, that is true in many local churches. The members see the pastor and staff as the "players" in ministry but view themselves as merely spectators. If the church is doing well, the members cheer. If the church begins to decline, the cheers quickly turn to jeers. That may make for exciting football, but it is a lousy way to run a church. Paul says God's pattern for the church is that every member be involved in ministry.

2. Every Christian has some nonoptional ministry responsibilities.

I had not been serving at one of my former churches long when one of the leaders invited me to lunch. "Pastor, you can ask me to do any number of things. But don't ask me to become involved in witnessing. That is not my gift," he warned in between bites of chips and hot sauce. He made the same mistake that many make: confusing giftedness with obedience. The Bible lists a number of ministry responsibilities that every Christian has:

We are to regularly share our faith with unbelievers (2
 Cor. 5:18-20; 1 Pet. 3:15).

We are to help new Christians become stronger in their
 faith (Matt. 28:19-20).

We are to pray for other Christians (James 5:16).

We are to share the burdens of other Christians (Gal.
 6:2).

We are to encourage other Christians (1 Thess. 5:11).

We are to meet the financial needs of less fortunate
 Christians (James 2:15-17).

We are to correct other Christians (Rom. 15:14).

These are nonoptional responsibilities for every believer,
though God may give us different ministries in which to fulfill
these basic responsibilities. Yet, as in the other subjects we have
addressed, I believe that the Christian culture has created some
myths about ministry that rob us of the joy of being able to say
"Enough. I have done everything I need to do."

Ministry Myth #1: "God desperately needs me, or his work won't get done."

Perhaps you have heard the words "God has no hands but
our hands, no feet but our feet, no voice but our voice." I
must confess I have even used those words before to shame
my members into ministry. Yet such an idea is contrary to the
words of Jesus, who said of his disciples, "I tell you, if these
[disciples] become silent, the stones will cry out!" (Luke
19:40).

Whenever I share my faith with a non-Christian, teach a
Sunday school class, or comfort a fellow believer who is dis-
tressed, I need to remember that although God has chosen to
use me as his spokesperson, the ultimate success of his eternal
purpose is not resting on my shoulders. What a relief!

Ministry Myth #2: "Ministry will free me from my personal problems" or "If you will quit focusing on yourself and instead concentrate on winning a lost world to Christ, you won't have time to think about your problems."

You have probably heard these lines before. There is an element of truth in them. Some people become so self-absorbed that they lose sight of their ministry responsibilities.

But churches are also filled with Christians who use ministry as an illegitimate escape from unresolved conflicts in their lives. Instead of dealing with the guilt of broken relationships with others, or even with God, they think that service in the church will atone for their sins and release them from their pain. Thus they are always trying to do more "for the Lord." Yet they can never seem to do enough.

God never intended for ministry to serve as an escape from problems. Jesus said that reconciling broken relationships with others is more important than ministry (Matt. 5:23-24). And David learned that God was more interested in our confronting our failures than in our offering sacrifices (Ps. 51:16-17).

Ministry Myth #3: "Ministry should take priority over my family."

Where in the world do people get this idea? Some people point to Jesus' words in Luke 14:26: "If anyone comes to Me, and does not hate his own father and mother and wife and children and brothers and sisters, yes, and even his own life, he cannot be My disciple." But it is clear from the passage that Jesus was not speaking of an emotional hatred toward one's family. Instead, he was using hyperbole to underscore the depth of our allegiance to God. How do I know that?

In chapter 10 we saw that one way to interpret difficult portions of Scripture is to compare them with other passages of

Scripture. As you search the Bible, you will see that Christians are commanded to care for the needs of their families:

> Husbands, love your wives, just as Christ also loved the church. . . . So husbands ought also to love their own wives as their own bodies. (Eph. 5:25, 28)

> The wife does not have authority over her own body, but the husband does; and likewise also the husband does not have authority over his own body, but the wife does. Stop depriving one another, except by agreement for a time that you may devote yourselves to prayer, and come together again lest Satan tempt you because of your lack of self-control. (1 Cor. 7:4-5)

> But if anyone does not provide for his own, and especially for those of his household, he has denied the faith, and is worse than an unbeliever. (1 Tim. 5:8)

> Behold, children are a gift of the Lord. (Ps. 127:3)

If our family is a gift from God, why would God ask us to destroy that which he has given us? Howard Hendricks says that the sacrifice of our family for ministry is a "bastard altar."

As we will see in the next section, one of our primary ministry responsibilities is with our family.

Ministry Myth #4: "Ministry must be painful to be worthwhile."

Some people point to David's words, "I will not offer burnt offerings to the Lord my God which cost me nothing" (2 Sam. 24:24), as a litmus test for ministry. If the ministry doesn't involve pain and sacrifice, God will not be pleased. You see this myth manifest itself in many ways:

- Christians who organize all-night prayer vigils, thinking God is impressed with their willingness to sacrifice sleep for prayer.
- Missionaries who choose the most remote and inconvenient part of the world to serve, convinced that God's will must involve sacrifice.
- Single adults who forfeit marriage "for the sake of the gospel."

Yes, we should be willing to make those sacrifices *if God asks us to make them.* But God is not always interested in sacrifice. Sometimes—in fact, most times—God's will is pleasant. Jesus said, "For My yoke is easy, and My load is light" (Matt. 11:30).

Ministry Myth #5: "Once I begin a ministry, I should never quit."

Again, some of the words of Jesus could lead one to believe this myth: "No one, after putting his hand to the plow and looking back, is fit for the kingdom of God" (Luke 9:62). Unfortunately, some Christians keep trying to plow ahead, even though the horse is dead!

Although we are always to be involved in ministry, sometimes the nature of our service changes. Consider the missionary who is called home because of health problems, or the Sunday school teacher who feels she is too old to be effective with high school girls, or the members of a church in a deteriorating section of town who are forced to relocate. Sometimes God uses circumstances to change our direction.

How can we gain a healthy, guilt-free perspective about ministry? Let me suggest four steps:

STEPS TO GUILT-FREE MINISTRY

1. Understand your unique place in the body of Christ.

The same dynamic that leads to an inability to relax contributes to guilt in ministry—the "If it's to be, it's up to me" syndrome. The apostle Paul offered an effective antidote to that attitude:

> For through the grace given to me I say to every man among you not to think more highly of himself than he ought to think; but to think so as to have sound judgment, as God has allotted to each a measure of faith. For just as we have many members in one body and all the members do not have the same function, so we, who are many, are one body in Christ, and individually members one of another. And since we have gifts that differ according to the grace given to us, let each exercise them accordingly: if prophecy, according to the proportion of his faith; if service, in his serving; or he who teaches, in his teaching; or he who exhorts, in his exhortation; he who gives, with liberality; he who leads, with diligence; he who shows mercy, with cheerfulness. (Rom. 12:3-8)

To paraphrase what Paul is saying here, "Relax. You can't do it all. The progress of the kingdom of God does not rest on your shoulders alone. God has given different Christians different gifts, and together they will accomplish God's purpose. Find your unique gift, and use it!"

I realize that spiritual gifts can be a cop-out for some ("I'm sorry, I would really like to contribute to the church's building program, but giving is not my gift.") But the Bible does teach that God has given you a unique gift for expressing his message to others. And it is through the exercise of your gift that you are going to derive the greatest satisfaction in ministry.

Recently, one of our laymen was asked to give a testimony in the morning worship service. He was petrified, although he did a tremendous job. Afterward he said to me, "Pastor, I don't see how you do what you do each week. I didn't realize the stress involved in standing before such a large crowd along with the bright lights and television cameras. I have a new appreciation for what you do each week." I thought to myself, *Stress? I love it! I can't wait for Sundays.* Why? Because the ability to do what was stressful for him is my gift. On the other hand, this same layman has a unique gift of exhortation. He is constantly ministering to young adults on a one-to-one basis. That kind of ministry would drive me crazy, but he loves it and is successful in it. Why? That is *his* unique gift.

Exercising our unique spiritual gifts not only brings us satisfaction, but it causes the body of Christ to function properly. Paul in other places used the same analogy of the human body:

> For even as the body is one and yet has many members, and all the members of the body, though they are many, are one body, so also is Christ. . . . If the whole body were an eye, where would the hearing be? If the whole were hearing, where would the sense of smell be? But now God has placed the members, each one of them, in the body, just as He desired. (1 Cor. 12:12, 17-18)

What could be a better picture of cooperation than the human body? The stomach feels hunger; the eyes spot a hamburger; the hands grab the burger, douse it with mustard, and shove it into the mouth; and it goes to the stomach, where its nutrition is processed and dispatched to the rest of the body. Now that is cooperation!

But imagine that your whole body were a giant eyeball. How would you ever take hold of the burger? What if your body were a giant ear? How would you ever digest the needed food? Just as the physical body is composed of many parts, so is the church. The proper functioning of the church (and the progress of the kingdom of God) depends on each member using his individual gift.

2. Refuse to compare your ministry with others'.

Failure to understand the concept of spiritual gifts results in one of two extremes—either you will think more highly of yourself than you should, or you will underestimate your importance in the kingdom of God. In Corinth, there were some believers who thought that their gifts were unimportant in the church. Perhaps these were people who could not preach, or teach, or perform other "up-front" ministries. Secretly, they coveted those more visible ministries.

But Paul reminded them that even if their ministry was not so visible, it was still vital to the body of Christ: "On the contrary, it is much truer that the members of the body which seem to be weaker are necessary; and those members of the body, which we deem less honorable, on these we bestow more abundant honor, and our unseemly members come to have more abundant seemliness, whereas our seemly members have no need of it" (1 Cor. 12:22-24).

Some of the human body's most vital organs are the least visible: the liver, the pancreas, the heart. Yet would anyone argue that they are unimportant? Paul says that it is the same in the body of Christ. That is why it is so foolish to compare our ministry to someone else's.

Recently I had lunch with a man who used to work in Christian radio. He served as a consultant for a number of well-known Christians. Many of his clients were heard on dozens, and even hundreds, of stations nationwide. Most ministers would give their right arm to have the kind of ministries these men had. Yet, he said, these men were dissatisfied with their radio ministries, because they were not as large as James Dobson's or Chuck Swindoll's. They felt guilty that they had not achieved a larger ministry.

Preachers are not the only people who are tempted to compare ministries. Maybe you wish you could teach like a gifted Bible scholar you have admired, or that you could sing like a soloist you have heard, or that you could serve on an important church committee like someone you know. Before you start comparing your ministry with others, remember that God has a unique blueprint for your life that includes your ministry. The psalmist expressed that truth when he wrote:

> You made all the delicate, inner parts of my body and knit them together in my mother's womb. . . . You saw me before I was born and scheduled each day of my life before I began to breathe. Every day was recorded in your book! (Ps. 139:13, 16, TLB)

3. See the ministry opportunities in your present circumstances.

George was a successful doctor in our church who had a real heart for ministry. He was actively involved in evangelism and discipleship ministries in our church, but he expressed a particular interest in foreign missions. One day he shared with me that he and his wife had applied to our denomination's mission board to serve as medical missionaries in Africa. I confess that I was disappointed over the prospect of losing such a gifted and dedicated couple from our fellowship.

A few months later they were rejected for service due to some medical problems. Naturally, they were extremely disappointed. Why wouldn't God allow them to serve him in such a substantial way? When I heard the news, I dropped by to see them, knowing they were hurting and perhaps in need of encouragement.

"What ministry would you be performing in Africa that you aren't able to do here?" I asked.

The doctor thought for a moment and answered, "Nothing, I guess." As we talked further, he began to see that God had not closed the door for missionary service. He was surrounded by just as many lost people or immature Christians in our community as would be in Africa. From that point on, he began to view his present circumstances as his ministry field.

Paul was a master at seeing ministry opportunities in whatever circumstance he found himself. While imprisoned in Rome, Paul wrote to the Philippians:

> Now I want you to know, brethren, that my circumstances have turned out for the greater progress of the gospel, so that my imprisonment in the cause of Christ has become well known throughout the whole praetorian guard and to everyone else, and that most of the brethren, trusting in the Lord because of my imprisonment, have far more courage to speak the word of God without fear. (Phil. 1:12-14)

God had called Paul to a worldwide ministry of sharing the gospel with the Gentiles. Yet Paul found himself imprisoned while others were experiencing spectacular ministries. What was Paul's response to his adverse circumstances? He could have become bitter. "God, you have really screwed up! What about this worldwide ministry you promised me?"

But instead of throwing a gigantic pity party for himself, he used his circumstances to further the gospel, diligently proclaiming the gospel message to the Roman soldiers guarding him. They, in turn, shared it with others until the message had spread through the entire "praetorian guard"—that unique group of soldiers who guarded Caesar's household. Instead of asking God to change his circumstances, Paul used his circumstances for ministry.

When I first felt God's call to enter the ministry, I went to visit my pastor, Dr. W. A. Criswell. Knowing that in a few years I would be going to college and then seminary, he offered this valuable advice: "Son, don't ask God to give you a ministry some time in the future. Make a ministry wherever you are."

I would offer the same advice to you. Instead of yearning for "a ministry" someplace or sometime in the future, view your family, your job, your school, or your neighborhood as the ministry field God has given you now.

4. Realize that you are not responsible for the response of others.

Whenever I conduct an evangelism training class at our church, one of the most frequently asked questions is this: "How do you personally deal with those who reject the gospel?" I always appreciate the question, because it reveals the primary reason more people don't share their faith regularly: We are afraid of rejection—nobody likes it. We all know the pain of being turned down for a date, or not asked to the prom, or not selected for a team, or skipped over for a promotion. For many people, volunteering for ministry is like wearing a giant Kick Me sign on our back. We are inviting pain. What if

- my neighbor says no to my invitation to become a Christian,
- my Sunday school class that I teach votes to disband after my first week,
- my friend that I counsel with refuses to follow my advice?

The good news is that God does not hold you responsible for how others respond to your ministry. When you faithfully share Christ's message with others—either through words or deeds—you have done your part. How the message is received is dependent upon the heart condition of the other person. How do I know that?

Remember Jesus' parable about the four soils in Matthew 13? A sower went out and widely scattered the seed, which fell on four different types of soil. Some of it fell on the hard soil by the road, some fell on shallow soil, some fell on weed-infested soil, and still other seed fell on good soil. The only seed that grew and bore fruit was that which fell on the good soil. Jesus went on to explain that the seed represented the Word of God, the sower represented anyone who shared the gospel, and the soils represented different conditions of the human heart. Only a heart that is receptive to the gospel will receive the gospel.

As "sowers" of the gospel message, we don't need to create the "seed" we are to spread—the message has already been given to us. Nor do we need to worry about our technique in spreading the seed—the sower in the parable certainly didn't. Our only responsibility is to spread the message. The response to our message depends upon the hearer.

If you are a pastor, then you can quit judging the success of your sermon by the response to the altar call. If you are a Sunday school teacher, you can quit judging the effectiveness of your ministry by the response of your students. If you are counseling a friend, you can quit judging your ability as a counselor by whether or not your friend follows your advice. Your responsibility is only to sow the seed. As long as you are regularly spreading the message of Christ through whatever gift God has given you, you can expect to hear God say one day, "Well done, good and faithful servant."

And isn't that the bottom line of guilt-free living—knowing that we have met God's expectations for our lives?

Last Saturday I decided to teach my oldest daughter how to ride a bicycle. She had been after me for months to do so, since most of her friends had already mastered the skill. As we took the bike out in the driveway, I frantically tried to remember how my father had taught me. Yet, in spite of my inadequacies as a teacher, I was amazed at how well she did for her first attempt. She fell down a lot, but she was staying up for longer and longer periods of time.

But that wasn't good enough for her. After an hour, she reached the point of ultimate frustration. She threw her bike down and ran into the house crying. My heart broke for her. I knew she was being too hard on herself. I followed her into her room and sat down by her side. "Honey, why are you so upset?" I asked. "You were doing great."

She replied, "But I wish I had done better. I'll never learn to ride like my friends. I quit." From her perspective she had failed because she hadn't mastered her bicycle. From my point of view, she had done a terrific job.

As we consider all of the life areas we have examined in this book—time management, marriage, parenting, and our spiritual lives—it is easy to focus on our deficiencies. We're trying to follow God's requirements in these areas, yet we wish we were doing better. As we compare ourselves to others, we are tempted to say, "I quit."

But I believe that if God were to sit down by our side and wrap his arms around us, most of us would be shocked to hear him say, "You're doing great. Quit being so hard on yourself."

Wishful thinking? Only for those who have allowed themselves to become slaves to the expectations of others. Once you understand—and apply—God's simple standards for each life area, you will be able to "go, then, eat your bread in happiness,

241

and drink your wine with a cheerful heart; [knowing that] God has already approved your works."

Go ahead, Solomon urged. Unshackle yourself from the expectations of others. Follow God's simple guidelines for living, and begin to enjoy a guilt-free life!

NOTES

Chapter One: *Enough Is Enough*

1. Harold Kushner, *When All You've Ever Wanted Isn't Enough* (New York: Pocket Books, 1986), 146.
2. Tim Hansel, *When I Relax I Feel Guilty* (Elgin, Ill.: David C. Cook Publishing Co., 1979), 44–45.

Chapter Two: *The Enemies of Guilt-Free Living*

1. John F. MacArthur, *The MacArthur New Testament Commentary: Romans 1–8* (Chicago: Moody Press, 1991), 178.

Chapter Three: *Guilt-Free Time Management*

1. Kushner, *All You've Ever Wanted*, 158–159.
2. Bobb Biehl, *Masterplan Your Life in One Day* (Laguna Niguel, Calif.: Masterplanning Group International, 1985), 6.
3. R. Alec Mackenzie, *The Time Trap* (New York: McGraw-Hill Book Company, 1972), 38–39.
4. Ted Engstrom used this poem in one of his "Managing Your Time" seminars in San Diego, California, in September, 1983. Source unknown.

Chapter Four: *Guilt-Free Work*

1. David McKenna, *Love Your Work* (Wheaton, Ill.: Victor Books, 1990), 15.
2. Diane Fassel, *Working Ourselves to Death* (San Francisco: Harper San Francisco, 1990), 44.
3. Ibid.
4. McKenna, *Love Your Work*, 35–38.
5. Ibid., 13.
6. Some of the ideas in this section were gleaned from the excellent book by Doug Sherman and William Hendricks, *Your Work Matters to God* (Colorado Springs: NavPress, 1987).
7. *Money* (April 1992): 146.
8. McKenna, 35.
9. John Gardner, *Excellence*, rev. ed. (New York: W. W. Norton, 1987).
10. McKenna, *Love Your Work*, 131.

11. Fassel, *Working*, 35.
12. Ibid., 14

Chapter Five: *Guilt-Free Relaxation*

1. Hansel, *I Feel Guilty*, 28.
2. Robert Jeffress, *Choose Your Attitudes, Change Your Life* (Wheaton, Ill.: Victor Books, 1992), 71
3. Ibid., 72.
4. Fassel, *Working*, 2.
5. Douglas Sherman and William Hendricks, *Your Work Matters to God* (Colorado Springs: NavPress, 1987), 37–38.
6. Jim Conway, *Men in Midlife Crisis* (Elgin, Ill.: David C. Cook Publishing Co., 1978), 66.
7. James D. Schwartz, *Enough* (Englewood, Colo.: Labrador Press, 1992), 13.
8. Greg Asimakoupoulos, John Maxwell, and Steve McKinley, *The Time Crunch: What to Do When You Can't Do It All* (Sisters, Ore.: Multnomah Books, 1993), 22.
9. Gordon MacDonald, *Ordering Your Private World* (Nashville: Oliver-Nelson, 1984), 162.
10. Ibid.
11. Jeffress, *Choose Your Attitudes*, 51.
12. The three sources of worry are adapted from chapter 4 of my book *Choose Your Attitudes, Change Your Life.*
13. Charles R. Swindoll, *Hand Me Another Brick* (Nashville: Thomas Nelson Publishers, 1978), 142.
14. Harvey Mackay, *Beware the Naked Man Who Offers You His Shirt* (New York: William Morrow and Company, Inc., 1990), 157.

Chapter Six: *Guilt-Free Money Management*

1. Joe Dominguez and Vicki Robin, *Your Money or Your Life* (New York: Penguin Books, 1993).
2. *Worth*, June 1993, 11.
3. *Money* (April 1992): 7.
4. Larry Burkett, *Debt-Free Living* (Chicago: Moody Press, 1989), 8.
5. Merrill C. Tenney, ed., *The Zondervan Pictorial Encyclopedia of the Bible*, vol. 5 (Grand Rapids: Zondervan Publishing House, 1977), 543.
6. Dominguez and Robin, *Your Money or Your Life*, 6.

Chapter Seven: *Guilt-Free Marriage*

1. Robert Jeffress, 147.
2. Dennis Rainey, *Lonely Husbands, Lonely Wives* (Dallas: Word, Inc., 1989), 14–15.

3. *U. S. News and World Report*, July 6, 1992, 62.

4. Ibid.

5. Richard J. Foster, *The Challenge of the Disciplined Life* (San Francisco: Harper San Francisco, 1985), 103.

6. Rainey, *Lonely Husbands*, 255.

7. Ibid., 82.

8. Bill and Lynne Hybels, *Fit to Be Tied* (Grand Rapids: Zondervan Publishing House, 1991), 43.

9. James Patterson and Peter Kim, *The Day America Told the Truth* (New York: Prentice Hall Press, 1991), 94.

10. Chuck Swindoll, *Newsbreak*, newsletter of the First Evangelical Free Church, Fullerton, Calif., June 14–20, 1992.

11. James Dobson, Focus on the Family newsletter, June 1991, 2–3.

12. James Dobson, *Love for a Lifetime* (Portland, Ore.: Multnomah Press, 1987), 98–99.

13. James Dobson, *Straight Talk to Men and Their Wives* (Waco, Tex.: Word, Inc., 1980), 71–72.

14. Lawrence J. Crabb, *The Marriage Builder* (Grand Rapids: Zondervan Publishing House, 1982), 20.

Chapter Eight: *Guilt-Free Parenting*

1. Tim Hansel, *What Kids Need Most in a Dad* (Old Tappan, N.J.: Fleming H. Revell Company, 1984), 33.

2. David Jeremiah, *Exposing the Myths of Parenthood* (Dallas: Word, Inc., 1988), 82.

3. Brian Harbor's newsletter, "Brian's Lines," April 1989, 5.

4. Chap Clark, *The Performance Illusion* (Colorado Springs: NavPress, 1993), 40.

5. James Dobson *Dare to Discipline* (Wheaton, Ill.: Tyndale House Publishers, 1970), 29.

6. Denis Waitley, *Seeds of Greatness* (Old Tappan, N.J.: Fleming H. Revell Company, 1983), 73.

7. Joe Temple, *Know Your Child* (Grand Rapids: Baker Book House, 1974), 93.

8. Clark, *Performance Illusion*, 30.

9. Tim Kimmel, *Raising Kids Who Turn Out Right* (Sisters, Ore.: Multnomah Press, 1989), 190.

10. Jeremiah, *Myths of Parenthood*, 28–29.

Chapter Nine: *Guilt-Free Friendships*

1. Charles R. Swindoll, *Living on the Ragged Edge* (Waco, Tex.: Word, Inc., 1985), 134.
2. Lloyd Cory, *Quotable Quotations* (Wheaton, Ill.: Victor Books, 1985), 146.
3. Joseph Bayly, *The Last Thing We Talk About* (Elgin, Ill.: David C. Cook Publishing Co., 1973), 55–56.
4. Jerry White and Mary White, *Friends and Friendship* (Colorado Springs: NavPress, 1982), 40.
5. Ted W. Engstrom, *Motivation to Last a Lifetime* (Grand Rapids: Zondervan Publishing House, 1984), 85–86.
6. Charles C. Ryrie, ed., *The Ryrie Study Bible*, New American Standard Translation (Chicago: Moody Press, 1976), 1880.

Chapter Ten: *Guilt-Free Bible Study*

1. Howard G. Hendricks and William D. Hendricks, *Living by the Book* (Chicago: Moody Press, 1991), 9–10.
2. Ibid., 10.
3. Ibid., 12.
4. Susan Simko, *The Baptist Standard*, 10 November 1993, 1.
5. In *Living by the Book*, Dr. Hendricks suggests five steps to correct interpretation: Content, Context, Comparison, Culture, and Consultation.
6. D. Edmond Hiebert, *The Epistle of James* (Chicago: Moody Press, 1979), 174–175.

Chapter Eleven: *Guilt-Free Praying*

1. Gordon MacDonald, *Private World*, 154.
2. R. Kent Hughes, *Disciplines of a Godly Man* (Wheaton, Ill.: Crossway Books, 1991), 95.
3. John MacArthur, Jr., *The Disciples' Prayer* (Panorama City, Calif.: Word of Grace Communications, 1981), 11.
4. Hughes, *A Godly Man*, 96.
5. David L. Goetz, "How Pastors Practice the Presence," *Leadership*, (fall 1993): 31.
6. Clark, *Performance Illusion*, 50.